T0128268

THE RISE OF THE
PROPHETIC
VOICE

ALPH LUKAU

BALBOA.PRESS

A DIVISION OF HAY HOUSE

Balboa Press books may be ordered through booksellers or by contacting:

Balboa Press
A Division of Hay House
1663 Liberty Drive
Bloomington, IN 47403
www.balboapress.com
1 (877) 407-4847

Print information available on the last page.

ISBN: 978-1-9822-3758-5 (sc)
ISBN: 978-1-9822-3760-8 (hc)
ISBN: 978-1-9822-3759-2 (e)

Library of Congress Control Number: 2019917167

Balboa Press rev. date: 10/24/2019

THE RISE OF THE PROPHETIC VOICE

The Rise of the Prophetic Voice is an educational and revolutionary book that deals with biblical truths about the prophetic and its practical operation in our time. This book is a rare tool of the Holy Spirit, dedicated to shedding light about the prophetic to the body of Christ and to raising an end-time army of prophets for the Lord.

The prophetic is the oldest and most documented ministry in the Bible, yet it is the least known in today's generation. No other ministry is known to be more effective in the Kingdom of God than the prophetic. The Bible, the most sacred book we have in the Kingdom of God, is a prophetic book; the birth of our Lord and Saviour Jesus Christ was a fulfilment of a prophetic word. God is restoring the prophetic in the church and calling all His sons and daughters to be prophetic.

The world today glorifies individualism and independence from God as a pathway to freedom, rendering the very essence of God irrelevant. However, the well-informed, Spirit-led and powerful revelations in *Rise of the Prophetic Voice* demonstrate God's unfailing power and establish His supremacy amongst men once again.

This book will give you the biblical foundation of the prophetic, help you to discover your calling or gift in it and ignite in you its fire. Beyond all doubt, I believe this book will revolutionise the lives of its readers and restore the glory of the mighty God in the world.

Nothing gives me greater joy than to be a blessing in ministry to someone.

In obedience to the Holy Spirit I wrote this book, trusting that whoever reads it will be edified, educated and empowered in the knowledge of the prophetic.

I dedicate this book to the AMI family, and to all those who are called to the prophetic ministry. This is your book. May it take you higher in God and prepare you for the end-time prophetic assignment of the church on earth.

With love Alph Lukau

Contents

INTRODUCTION

> ### HOSEA 12:13*
>
> By a prophet the LORD brought Israel out of Egypt, and by a prophet he was preserved.

Martin Luther King Jr. once said,

> If the church does not recapture its prophetic zeal,
> it will become an irrelevant social club without any
> moral or spiritual authority.†

More than ever, the church of our Lord Jesus Christ today needs its prophetic voice restored. The purpose of the church on earth is truly not to be merely a social movement of people who adhere to certain set rules of good behaviour. The church is rather a body of those who are saved by the precious blood of Jesus Christ and appointed to be His representatives in the world. The mission of the church is to make Christ known through the demonstration of his power and glory, in preaching and living the Word of God.

The church is called upon not only to preach the gospel but also to live that very gospel. To preach the gospel means to proclaim the message of the gospel, the Word of God, and to live the gospel means to experience that message personally. If I proclaim to the world that Jesus Christ is the same yesterday, today, and forever more, I must be able to experience that very truth in my own personal life. If I

---

* Unless otherwise indicated, all biblical citations are from the New King James Version (NKJV).

† Martin Luther King, Jr., "A Knock at Midnight," June 5, 1963 https:// kinginstitute. stanford. edu/king-papers/documents/knock-midnight

proclaim that Jesus heals, I must be able to experience His healing power in my life and through my life. If I proclaim that miracles are the bread of and for God's children, I must also be able to witness those miracles in my life today. I should be able to see them happening throughout my life.

It is unfortunate that the church of God is fast losing its spiritual identity and the gospel is losing its position of power in the world. Today, the church is seen as more of a social club of like-minded people, whose gatherings have less and less spiritual impact in the real world. In a greater sense, the church has lost its crucial identity as a *spiritual body*. In many countries, churches are legally categorised as cultural rather than spiritual entities; in other words, churches are legally registered as cultural organisations. I don't blame the legislatures for this legal definition; they have categorised the church based on the facts and evidence before them.

The church of our Lord Jesus Christ should not be limited to the role of a cultural organisation. A church can function culturally as a place of motivation, where we learn decent behaviour. There, we may even discuss Bible stories and practise devotion and meditation for inner peace. Even so, we would miss the real gospel. We need to regain the fire of God in the church. Let us arise to take back our rightful place as a spiritual body of power so that we may establish the kingdom of God in this world.

People and nations today need to experience the power of God through the church, and the prophetic voice is the means through which God is restoring to the church the power of the gospel. Without God's prophetic move, confusion and darkness will continue to hover over the face of the earth. The prophetic is like the ignition, which gets the church moving again. Prophecy will restore the church to its original identity and bring back the fire of God. Deliverance will come to the people of this world.

The Rise of the Prophetic Voice

Hosea reports, "By a prophet, the LORD brought Israel out of Egypt, and by a prophet he was preserved" (Hos 12:3). Here, Hosea is saying that the Lord, through the prophet, delivered the people during the Exodus from slavery in Egypt. Furthermore, the prophet has preserved Israel. So shall it be in our time. God will bring deliverance through prophecy; God will also preserve His people, the church, through His servants, the prophets. Please note that God does not change and neither have God's methods. Just as God used the prophet for the deliverance and preservation of Israel, His people, in former times, so will He use His anointed servants, the prophets, to establish His perfect will and to deliver His people in our times and for our own generation.

The Lord has mandated that I write this book to prepare the church and His people to make ready for the return of the prophetic to the church today. *I am a prophet of God.* This book is written under the prophetic guidance of the Holy Spirit. Enriched by a great wealth of theological knowledge, this book contains a treasure house of fundamental biblical teachings.

We are indeed living in different times now as compared to our forefathers. In our times, God will move through prophecy, for the prophetic is an end-of-time ministry. The prophetic is the last weapon of the Lord to bring and to demonstrate His power in this world. *The prophetic is the Lord's last card.* There is a strong prophetic wind of the Holy Spirit blowing in the world today; unless the church is informed and prepared, we will miss the doings of the Lord completely.

I write this book in full submission to the Spirit of God and with the sole purpose of making a significant contribution to what the Lord Himself is already doing in the church. This book will present you with the fundamental biblical truths about the prophetic; it will enlighten your mind through insight. You will gain the ability to respond to and be embraced by God's prophetic move.

I saw in a vision that millions of people around the world were arising with a strong prophetic mantle upon them. I saw infants prophesying. I saw a boy and girl – mere children – a multicultural army of young people, both ordinary believers and ministers alike; all were arising strong in the prophetic spirit. The world is already vibrating with the arising of God's prophetic move. The spirit of prophecy will grow and spread like wildfire – it will not stop. From the South to the North and the East to the West, every part of the globe will experience the arising of prophets, sprouting like mushrooms. Prophets will speak to this world on behalf of the Lord.

This book is a strategic tool of the Holy Spirit to awaken, to educate, to equip and to prepare the church of God for the arising of the prophetic. I pray that the prophetic flames of fire may be ignited in you as you read. Therefore, keep an open mind as you read, and allow the Spirit of God directly to minister to you.

Schools of Theology

We are caught between many schools of theology in the church. Excessive debates have sown confusion in the Body of Christ, clouding our understanding of the mind of God in the Scriptures. As a result, there are many divisions among us.

We use the same Bible and we read the same biblical verses, but we differ tremendously in our interpretations. A state of darkness is occurring because the light of the prophetic has been extinguished among many in the Body of Christ. We try to understand and to interpret the Word of God through the strength of our intellect rather than by the revelation of the Holy Spirit.

The Rise of the Prophetic Voice

Today, amongst the different schools of theology, we have three groups with different lines of thoughts and beliefs:

1. The prophetic, along with the gifts of the Holy Spirit (and certain biblical ministries), no longer exist in our time.
2. The prophetic, along with all the biblical gifts and ministries, was given to the church. So long as the church exists on earth, the prophetic will remain in operation and the gifts of the Holy Spirit will continue to belong to us.
3. The prophetic ministry, and the gifts of the Spirit, are all in operation in the church today, but they no longer operate like they used to in earlier times.

Theological and Historical Overview

Before outlining these three schools of theology in general terms, let me provide a brief historical overview of the positions in Christianity with regard to miracles and charismatic gifts. Please note that my remarks are intended by way of a general overview.* Deeper scholarly exposition would, of course, complicate this picture.

Historically, the mainline Protestant denominations, especially Lutherans and Calvinists, believed that all of nature is infused by the Spirit of God. God acts through doctors and natural medicines for healing, and through people and situations in ordinary and extraordinary ways. In practice, these denominations have tended to be suspicious of healing and miracles that claim supernatural causality.

---

* For a good overview of the role of miracles and charismatic phenomena in mainline and historical Christianity, see Peter L. Berger, "A Friendly Dissent from Pentecostalism," November 2012. https://www. firstthings. com/ article/2012/11/a-friendly-dissent-from-pentecostalism

In Catholicism, the Eucharist itself and the sacraments make the presence of God real. Catholics also admit that saints and holy people do miracles, as does Mary, the mother of God. These miracles must be verified by an ecclesiastical commission.

Even though these mainstream Christian denominations do not always give a big role to miracles, healings, and inspired prophecies in their congregations today, there are charismatic revival movements within them.

The Protestant churches, in response to Pentecostalism, have developed more recently a doctrine that they call cessationism.* It is this cessationist idea that is my main point of focus in the arguments I offer on behalf of the prophetic ministry and the gifts of the Spirit (including miracles and healing).

I refer to the supernatural throughout this book. By "supernatural," I mean that God, heaven, or the divine are the causal agents of a given speech act or deed. The supernatural causality may work by human agency and intermediaries. However, the causality belongs to God in a realm beyond the natural.

First Group: Supernatural gifts of the Spirit are for the early church exclusively

This group believes that the prophetic, along with the gifts of the Holy Spirit (and certain biblical ministries), no longer exist in our time. For this group, all such spiritual phenomena ceased when the biblical prophets and the apostles died. In brief, according to this view, the prophetic, along with the gifts of the Holy Spirit and certain ministries, were limited to the apostles and prophets mentioned in

---

* For some of the debates, see this article: Jon Ruthven,"Answering the Cessationists' Case against Continuing Spiritual Gifts," *Pneuma*, Vol. 3.2, 2000.

the Bible. They believe those ministries and gifts were important for an earlier time only. The gifts of the Spirit are not for this dispensation since Jesus has already fulfilled all spiritual work on the Cross.

For example, these theologians see no reason why God should still speak through prophets since we have all been saved and we have Jesus Christ in our lives. So, unlike in the olden days, where people had neither Jesus nor the Holy Spirit in their lives, we are now privileged to have a direct line to God. We can hear Him for ourselves without needing anyone to speak on God's behalf. When we are sick, we do not need anyone to administer a healing ministry upon us because we can call on Jesus directly for our healing.

Though this argument may sound logical, its truth is incomplete, misleading, and indeed very dangerous. The coming of Christ in our dispensation does not imply the abolition of the prophetic and the apostolic ministry in and for the church today. Remember, we are the Body of Christ (1 Cor 12:12, 27). In every body, organs are given vital roles for the betterment and health of the body. The work of Christ on the Cross of Calvary does not remove men and women from having useful roles in the operation of Christ's Body (the *church*); on the contrary, the Cross has given a new meaning and purpose to our ministries.

We are often under the impression that, because we are saved and reconciled with the Father, we need no one else in our relationship with God except the Holy Spirit. This is a misconception. It is true that Jesus Christ has fulfilled the requirements for our salvation, and Jesus Christ is the only mediator between the Father and us. However, Christ's work does not remove the role of men and women from our walk with God; on the contrary, Christ has established a more effective mandate in our lives so that we may depend on Christ's ministers in our own day, both prophets and apostles.

Understand that God uses people to bless us, and He has selected and anointed people as his tool to fulfil that blessing. Through those that God has selected and anointed, He teaches us His Word, He builds our faith, and He releases blessings in our lives. Through them, God speaks to us and takes us deeper into His presence. Note that it is God Who is doing all of these things while using different tools. God appoints and anoints men and women for the job. This policy is consistent with the Scriptures and the teachings of the apostles. In 1 Cor 12:28-29, the apostle Paul outlines the different roles in the church, including prophets. Similarly, in the Epistles, the prophetic is mentioned in the list of the fivefold ministry, given as gifts from Christ.

> ### EPH 4:11
>
> And He Himself gave some *to be* apostles; and some prophets; and some evangelists; and some pastors and teachers.

Notice that *prophets* are ministers of Christ, just like evangelists, pastors, teachers and apostles. They are all men and women, divinely selected and anointed to minister to us. Ephesians 4 tells us that their work or assignment in our lives is useful for the perfection of the saints and for the edification of the Body of Christ:

> ### EPH 4:13
>
> Till we all come in the unity of the faith, and of the knowledge of the Son of God, unto a perfect man, unto the measure of the stature of the fullness of Christ.

The book of Acts speaks of a prophet named Agabus who was used by the Holy Spirit to minister to Paul. The prophet Agabus prophesied to Paul, warning him of events that were to come onto his path.

> ### ACTS 21:10 – 11
>
> And as we stayed many days, a certain prophet named Agabus came down from Judea. When he had come to us, he took Paul's belt, bound his *own* hands and feet, and said: "Thus says the Holy Spirit, so shall the Jews at Jerusalem bind the man who owns this belt, and deliver *him* into the hands of the Gentiles."

Here we see that even Paul the apostle, who is best known amongst biblical scholars as the supreme figure of the New Testament, was a beneficiary of the prophetic ministry. This should inform us of the validity and veracity of the prophetic ministry in our dispensation.

Agabus was a New Testament prophet of the Lord; he was born-again and Spirit-filled. His ministry was in revealing what was yet to come. Not only do we see him here prophesying to Paul, but the Bible reports that he predicted a severe famine which, the author of Acts says, occurred during the reign of the Roman Emperor Claudius.

> ### ACTS 11:28
>
> Then one of them, named Agabus, stood up and showed by the Spirit that there was going to be a great famine throughout the entire world, which also happened in the days of Claudius Caesar.

The Bible, in the New Testament, lists the prophetic ministry in the five-fold ministry; so, to believe that the prophetic ministry is part of the Old Testament and no longer relevant to us today suggests that pastors, evangelists and teachers are part of the past ministries too, and are not relevant to us today. If that is so, which ministry will remain to serve the Body of Christ?

Second Group: The supernatural gifts of the Spirit exist for all time in the Church

This group's belief system is in the right place; they believe correctly. They believe that the prophetic gifts, along with all the biblical ministries, were given to the church. As long as the church exists on earth, the prophetic, the gifts of the Holy Spirit, and all the biblical ministries, will remain in operation; they are of paramount importance for the survival of the church in our generation.

Those who fall in this category of thinking and believing are often considered radical, crazy, fanatics, unreal and deluded. Their revelation and faith set them apart from the rest. They are normally judged, rejected and persecuted by their own, simply because they come across as weird in their beliefs and actions. Yet they are the only group from the three main schools of theology that is on the correct path.

God is looking for this group of believers for the end-time assignment, in the world and in the church alike.

Third Group: The supernatural gifts of the Spirit exist with diminished potency

This group believes that the prophetic ministry and the gifts of the Spirit remain in operation in the church today, but that these gifts no longer operate in our own times in the same manner as they used to operate in the past. This group seems to advocate that *the ministries and gifts of the Holy Spirit have lost their original functions*. Though they are still in the church today, they are milder and not as vigorous in their manifestations and operations.

For example, according to this group the prophetic ministry today is reduced to a word of encouragement between brothers; prophecy is no longer based on revelation of mysteries or an accurate prediction of future events. Prophecy amounts now to good, edifying words given to one another. *For example*, Brother *Willy* tells brother *Roberto* to remain strong amidst his difficulties because God is with him. *Madeleine* tells *Margaret* that the sun will shine again tomorrow and that God's love for her is unfailing. Please note that such words from amongst brethren are great and very edifying, but they do not in any way constitute a prophetic word. *What makes a prophecy is far beyond the good and edifying words that we may have for one another.*

Given all of these different understandings and interpretations of the concept of prophecy, it's clear that the church of God is extremely divided by many opinions and schools of thought. This division is proving to be dangerous. *The many opinions weaken the Body of Christ and cause unnecessary strife.* Due to a lack of true understanding about the prophetic, and the operation of the gifts of the Spirit in the church, the power of God is literally rejected, in large part, by the church itself. More and more, we see the church of our Lord Jesus Christ building its comfort and safety by its routines and the traditions of earlier times.

Instead of opening up to the revelation of God in what God is doing in our times now, a vast part of the church of God finds it too risky and adventurous to be open. They would rather remain in what is familiar, conventional and secure. Whatever has been mastered and grandly accepted by all seems preferable to a daring exercise of faith in the manifestations of the power of God, which are promised and stipulated in the Scriptures.

Pastor Jacques A. Vernaud repeatedly used to say in the pulpit,

> Many churches around the world have mastered the
> running of our Sunday worship services, so much
> so that even when the Holy Spirit is absent no one
> will notice its absence.*

This observation may sound scandalous, but it is shockingly true. Today, most churches do not need the Holy Spirit for anything because they seem to have everything under control. In many instances, if the Holy Spirit were to interrupt a programme in one of our churches or to lead people in a specific and different direction or to assign them to a different task, the people and church leadership would rebuke the Holy Spirit and unequivocally reject the instruction – all of this because we are largely slaves of our routines and traditions. We naturally reject whatever does not fit into this world as we know it. At the very root of this habit of complacency, in churches across the globe, is the tendency to attribute to the Devil the miraculous work of God.

I sometimes wonder if we still believe that God is more powerful than the Devil, for if we truly believed in the power of God we would always attribute any powerful manifestation of the supernatural to God rather than to the Devil. This point needs serious consideration. Many times, we have ostracised people and attributed the miracles that we see through them to the Devil instead of accepting that the miracles are God's doing. We have turned spiritually cold and sceptical; our faith is weak or sometimes non-existent, as if "having a form of godliness but denying its power" (2 Tim 3:5). We need more convincing today to accept that a miracle is from God rather than the Devil; what's worse is that ministers of the gospel today are more sceptical about the power of God than ordinary believers. This I say to our shame.

---

* This quote is based on the author's personal experience and direct acquaintance with Pastor Vernaud.

The Rise of the Prophetic Voice

The prophetic voice is the most misunderstood ministry in our era; pastors and ministers across the world have preached and taught against it openly in their churches, warning their congregations to stay away from prophecy completely. They have painted prophetic gifts to be works of evil, and they have accused those operating in the prophetic to be fraudsters or magicians while only pretending to be the servants of God. I certainly believe the critics would also have called *Moses* a magician if they had been there when he confronted the Pharaoh with the power of God to deliver Israel. They would have called *Shadrach, Meshach* and *Abednego* magicians since the power of God worked through them in Babylon (Daniel 3). They would have rejected the ministries of *Elijah, Elisha, Paul, Peter, Philip,* and even *Jesus himself,* together with the other remarkable charismatics of the past, whom God blessed mightily.

Most of those who stand up against the manifestation of the power of God today would have never believed in Jesus Christ if they had lived during the time He lived on earth. *They would have surely been like those who considered him to be a fraudster, a sinner and a magician* (e.g. see the demon accusation in John 10:20 and in Matt 12:24). Sceptics can believe in Jesus today so long as the stories in the Bible remain somehow abstract to them and can pass as myths; thus, these stories are no longer shocking to their belief systems.

Many argue that the reason behind this scepticism is the abuse and wrongdoing in the Body of Christ. Sceptics and unbelievers may have known someone who is a fraud, passing as a prophet of God, and such negative experiences have caused them to stand against the prophetic or the gifts of the Spirit.

It is unfortunate that there are fake prophets out there who may be causing havoc in the Body of Christ, just as it is unfortunate that there are fake pastors out there, fake evangelists, fake Christians, fake politicians, fake doctors, fake policemen, fake friends, fake bank notes, fake goods on the market, and so forth. The mere fact that one person is bad does not imply that all are bad. One bad experience ought not to cause one to paint everything and everyone else with the same brush. It is unwise to make such generalisations and also greatly regrettable. Though there are fake pastors, teachers, evangelists, prophets, and apostles out there, there are also genuine ones. In fact, it is important to note that the genuine ones are and will always be in greater number than the fake.

---

1 Kgs 19:18

Yet I have reserved seven thousand in Israel, all whose knees have not bowed to Baal, and every mouth that has not kissed him.

There are men and women of God (the "seven thousand" in the biblical passage) amongst those who are called in the prophetic and who operate with the power of God. They have not compromised their callings. They have not bowed to Baal; they remain genuine tools of God for the demonstration of His power.

The American biblical scholar, Michael Heiser, makes an astute critique of modern Christianity for its scepticism about the supernatural:

> Modern Christianity suffers from two serious shortcomings when it comes to the supernatural world.

> First, many Christians claim to believe in the supernatural but think and live like sceptics. We find talk of the supernatural world uncomfortable. This is typical of denominations and evangelical congregations outside the charismatic movement – in

The Rise of the Prophetic Voice

other words, those from a background like the one I grew up in.

There are two basic reasons why noncharismatics tend to close the door on the supernatural world. One is their suspicion that charismatic practices are detached from sound exegesis of Scripture. As a biblical scholar, it's easy for me to agree with that suspicion – but over time it has widely degenerated into closed-minded overreaction that is itself detached from the worldview of the biblical writers.

The other reason is less self-congratulatory. The believing church is bending under the weight of its own rationalism, a modern worldview that would be foreign to the biblical writers. Traditional Christian teaching has for centuries kept the unseen world at arm's length. We believe in the Godhead because there's no point to Christianity without it. The rest of the unseen world is handled with a whisper or a chuckle.

The second serious shortcoming is evident within the charismatic movement: the elevation of experience over Scripture. While that movement is predisposed to embrace the idea of an animate spiritual world, its conception of that world is framed largely by experience and an idiosyncratic reading of the book of Acts.*

---

* Michael S. Heiser, *The Unseen Realm: Recovering the Supernatural Worldview of the Bible*, (Bellingham, WA: Lexham Press, 2015), ch. 2. One can find here, too, his discussion of mental filters.

Heiser's critique has two components. Critics of the charismatic movement believe that charismatic phenomena lack grounding in sound biblical exegesis. They also suspect that charismatics may place experiences over obedience to Scripture. If experiences are their guide, they may be prone to many deviations from the Word of God.

While these two shortcomings seem very different, they are born from the same fundamental and underlying problem: modern Christianity's view of the supernatural is not framed by or in accord with the ancient worldview of the biblical writers. As Heiser sums up the problem:

> One segment wrongly consigns the invisible realm to the periphery of theological discussion. The other is so busy seeking some interaction with it that it has become unconcerned with its biblical moorings, resulting in a caricature.[*]

Though I am concerned about both shortcomings, the problem of the Christian sceptic is the greater hazard that now faces us.

The truth is that our modern church subculture, in its traditions, has trained us to suppose that our theology must preclude experiences of the supernatural. Consequently, such experiences are not an important part of church or biblical theology for many people. My contention is that, if our theology really derives from the biblical text, then we must reconsider our *selective supernaturalism* and recover a *biblical theology of the supernatural*. This is not to suggest that the best interpretation of a passage is always the most supernatural one. However, the biblical writers and those to whom they wrote were predisposed to supernaturalism. To ignore that outlook or to marginalise it will produce a biblical interpretation that reflects our

---

* Ibid.

The Rise of the Prophetic Voice

own sceptical mindset rather than the outlook of the biblical writers themselves, who were inspired by the Holy Spirit.

Rightly understood, the Bible is a prophetic book from start to finish, from Genesis to the Book of Revelation, and recounts many instances of the supernatural; most of the events contained in it are supernatural. For this reason, the biblical writers use words like "inspiration" and "revelation"; they are proof of the supernaturalism contained in the Bible.

Thepropheticvoiceasitismanifested inour time todayissupernatural and biblical.

> ### 1 COR 13:12B
> Now I know in part but then I shall know just as I also am known.

In this scripture of the apostle Paul, the statement "I know in part" suggests that no one has full knowledge of divine things all at once. Revelation and knowledge are given to us progressively. What we know today is not all that needs to be known. Paul is best known by biblical scholars as the supreme apostle of the New Testament, because of his vast knowledge and his many writings. If Paul says that we know only in part, we should all try to learn more, rather than playing as if we are the *know-it-all giants* of all truth that has ever been known and that will ever be known.

Those who try to reprimand others, based on what is beyond their mental library, act as if they know everything that needs to be known; therefore, they can discern what is of God and what is not of God without fear of contradiction. This arrogance is a big deception, and those with such attitudes perish in their pride. When you think you know all that needs to be known, you will become judgemental towards everything that you encounter. Your philosophy will likely be as follows: *unless it is done according to what you accept, it is not of God and should be rejected.*

With such an attitude, you will not feel the need to delve deeper into the Scriptures to discover the truth in a manner of inquiry and investigation. Nor will you consult the Spirit to reveal how to deal with what you are hearing or seeing. Your verdict will always come from your thoughts and not from the truth of the Word of God. The Pharisees and Sadducees who crucified Jesus operated with similar self-regard. They sincerely believed that they were guarantors of the truth of God, so much so that when Jesus Christ came to save humanity, they stood up against Him, cursed Him and hanged Him on the Cross. And this Jesus was the very Son of God (*the Word made flesh*).

The American writer, futurist, and businessman, Alvin Toffler, said,

> The illiterate of the 21st century will not be those who cannot read and write, but those who cannot learn, unlearn, and relearn.*

Those who have a learning heart do not reject things that they encounter on the pretext that they are not true. The learners do not cling to their own knowledge so as to remain in their comfort zones. Rather, they keep challenging their level of exposure and knowledge by studying the Word of God and opening themselves to the light of the Holy Spirit through prayer. They widely accept that there is much more to be known beyond the limits of their own knowledge. So, with an open mind, they continually enter into a quest for further knowledge.

---

* Alvin Toffler, *Future Shock*, 1970. Note that there is some question about the exact wording of this quote: https://www. oxfordreference. com/ view/10.1093/ acref/9780191826719.001.0001/q-oro-ed4-00010964

If we do not agree with someone about a particular revelation of the Word or a ministry practice, our disagreement does not necessarily imply that the practice is wrong, no matter how different or new it may seem to be. Understand that what may seem unusual to you may simply be unknown because it is a different revelation, as compared to what you already know. So instead of throwing away what is new entirely, simply because you have a different view, I suggest that you seek God with a humble heart so that God may reveal to you whether it is He who is at work or not.

The Bishop

A well-known bishop, with a congregation of around 20 000, shared with me his past struggle in accepting the prophetic move of God. He said he grew up in a school that taught him that *blue is blue, red is red,* and *black is black.* The line guarding what is true and acceptable was so rigidly defined that there could be no space for a different way of understanding reality. To him, there was only one way a pious woman was supposed to look and act in church; any woman who did not conform to this preconceived notion was disqualified from being *good,* irrespective of how piously they may have behaved. Even if she behaved well, she would still be considered a sinner and a hypocrite, who was just pretending to behave like a good woman. To this man, God operated in just one way; anything else was unacceptable and immediately deemed to be ungodly.

Once he learned of the manifestations of the power of God in the Body of Christ in our own times, this bishop at first believed that Satan was literally invading the church. So he took it upon himself to resist this apparent evil. He started preaching and teaching everywhere he went that those who operate in the supernatural domain are not to be trusted; they are fraudsters and do not serve God in truth. He made it his mission to warn the church against the supernatural. He was sincere and thought that he was being used by God to defend a right and holy cause. What he did not know was that he was being used to wound the Body of our Lord Jesus Christ and to persecute the prophets of God.

After coming across my ministry online, this man reluctantly began to watch our manifestations of the power of God, including accurate prophecies and evidence of their fulfilment. He watched testimonies of individuals who had experienced different kinds of miracles in their lives through our ministry. He said he listened to almost all of my sermons and my teachings. He even became addicted to watching them. The more he did so, the more his heart began to open. Yet, despite this opening, he still felt he was being seduced and brainwashed by my ministry. So he forced himself never to watch my programs again.

Three weeks after having pulled away from my ministry, he had a dream in which God rebuked him by making use of a scripture from Acts.

ACTS 10:15

And a voice *spoke* to him again the second time, "What God has cleansed you must not call common".

This dream marked for him the beginning of a U-turn away from his narrow-mindedness and toward the revelation of the Holy Spirit.

In the spiritual life, we may unlearn and relearn, because revelation is progressive. The church of God, as we know it today, has come a long way. In former times, if you laid hands on someone and he happened to fall on the ground under the power of the Holy Spirit, you might be regarded as a magician or a fraud. People might accuse you of simply pushing people to the ground by human force, so as to make the fall seem as if it had been caused by the action of the Holy Spirit. However, the practice of swooning or falling by the power of the Holy Spirit is more acceptable today. It has now been revealed to many that it is God's power that sometimes makes people fall. This is not to say that falling under the power of the Holy Ghost, or being "slain by the Spirit," is indispensable for receiving a blessing or miracle. But, at least today we have a better perspective on this phenomenon.

The church has grown in knowledge over the years. In former times, it was not acceptable for a woman to minister the Word of God from the church pulpit but, as we have grown in knowledge and revelation, God is using more and more great women as tools for the kingdom. As our knowledge in God and of God has evolved, so too has our worship, ministry and outlook. I often jokingly say that if God were to resurrect a few of our fathers in faith today and make them attend even some of our most conservative church services, they would probably return to their graves scandalised and in tears.

Not too long ago, for most of the Christian body, television was perceived to be an instrument of deception and propaganda, a tool of the Devil from which believers had to stay away or they would go to Hell. Some believers were expelled from their churches simply for watching television. Today, though, we not only have strong believers who are playing major roles in the media, but we also have church programmes on many television channels, both secular and Christian alike, across the globe. I believe that the prophetic will also gain widespread appeal, in our times today.

We should remember that revelation is progressive; what we did not know years ago will unfold and become clearer with time. Let us not be legalistic in our approach but rather open to the Holy Spirit's lead to enlighten us as to the truth of God's Word. *The science fiction of yesterday is our reality of today, and the science fiction of today will surely become our day-to-day reality of tomorrow.*

Spiritual Truths

Let us pause for a moment and think about the doctrine of the Trinity. When exactly did the church start to elaborate and embrace this doctrine? Do you know that there is no mention of the word *Trinity* in the Bible? Should we discount this entire doctrine because of this? This simple reflection may move us away from being blindly legalistic when it comes to the *logos* Word; (in this context, *logos* refers to the *written Word of God*). We may seek instead the revelation of the Spirit for a spiritual understanding. Although the exact word for *Trinity* does not appear in the Bible, as a concept it is manifested by the light of the Holy Spirit throughout the teachings of the Bible.

To refuse a *spiritual truth* on the pretext that is not in the Scriptures is dangerous. We need to be holistic and revelation-driven in our approach. For a long time, we were comfortable with the revelation that we had of the five-fold ministry. We were very comfortable when we referred to God's servants as pastors, evangelists, prophets, teachers and apostles. Since we had no difficulty recognising these ministries, there has been no discussion or debate about the five- fold ministry. It was accepted as a norm that a servant of God might be an evangelist, a prophet, a pastor, a teacher or an apostle.

It is imperative to assert that pastors, evangelists, prophets, teachers and apostles did not have any significant supernatural *authentication mark* that could clearly attest to the veracity of their calling. Although some in the five-fold ministry were mightily used by God in the demonstration of the supernatural power of the Holy Spirit, their charismatic gifts did not constitute an authentication of the office of their ministries.

The Rise of the Prophetic Voice

The prophetic is the only ministry amongst the five-fold ministry that bears a heavy and spectacular authentication mark of a supernatural kind. One gains the ability to hear what ears cannot hear, to see what human eyes cannot see, to know things by supernatural ability, and to predict with accuracy coming events. Unlike the rest of the five-fold ministry, many people have not wanted to associate themselves with the prophetic because the *visible authentication mark* was costly. So, many simply rejected the call of God in their lives or suppressed it to serve quietly by a less demanding calling.

A prophet does not merely give a word of encouragement or teach the Word, but instead prophesies with an accurate revelation. By the prophetic, God anoints His servant to literally speak in His name as a spokesperson. People will hold him accountable for his words in the name of the Lord. The demand on the prophetic ministry is so heavy that most would rather not be associated with it.

I heard someone criticising a prophet who, through an accurate revelation during the service, called out someone's name and told him things as the Lord revealed them to him. I heard his critics mocking him. They said that "mentioning someone's name by revelationdoes not mean much, and does not change anything". After allowing the critic to finish his line of thought, I asked him if he was truly able to perform the same kind of feat. He answered, "Calling someone's name accurately in the prophetic is not important. I am used to greater things than that in the kingdom."

So, I asked him to try to do the very thing that he had undermined in the ministry of that prophet – since he claimed to be called to greater things. I asked him to pick someone's name from the people around us, which he could not do accurately. That feat was clearly impossible for him. No one can call out someone's name unless he has a supernatural ability. One cannot prophesy accurately unless one has supernatural ability, endowed by the Spirit of God. So, I urged him to stop undermining the things he was not able to do himself.

Many ministers of the gospel run away from the prophetic ministry and turn against it for fear of being measured by it. While concealing their inability in prophecy, they wage war on the very genuineness of the prophetic ministry.

The prophetic is not like the task of preaching a good sermon, only to vanish afterwards; in the prophetic, you are meant to be the voice of the Lord, and your words will be tested. People will wait for the fulfilment of whatever you have prophesied. There is great pressure put on the prophetic ministry, which tends to scare away many who are called to it. They shy away from being called prophets, or from associating with prophecy in any way whatsoever, since they fear being held to or measured by its exacting standards. And such fears should dissolve because, when God calls you, He equips you Himself. All you have to do is avail yourself of His call. Remember: *God does not call the qualified; He qualifies the called.* If you avail yourself of His call, He will anoint. He will guide and train you Himself. *It always seems impossible until it is done.*

The mere fact that you are reading this book is a set-up to challenge you to open up to God and to be part of the army of those who are used in the prophetic, be it in your home, your career, your community, or in some other way by which you are to respond to this calling in your local church.

The Prophetic

Much debate about the prophetic is taking place in this era in which the prophetic is clearly being restored. Many have attributed the entire ministry of the prophetic to demons, and prophets have been called a lot of derogatory names; they have been demonised because they speak on God's behalf. Prophets around the world have been put on trial by other ministers simply because they are prophets; they have all been tarred and feathered with the same brush. If we believe that there are pastors, evangelists, teachers and apostles, why not believe that there are prophets?

EPH 4:11

And He Himself gave some *to be* apostles, some prophets, some evangelists, and some pastors and teachers.

It is interesting that we accept some parts of this verse and reject others. Please understand that the prophetic is the voice of God for our time. The prophetic is not meant to compete with other ministries in the Body of Christ but rather to fulfil them. With the rise of the prophetic voice, I believe that the five-fold ministry is now complete. There is a need to clarify that it is God Himself who calls people. None of the genuine ministers of the gospel have called themselves into the ministry.

AMOS 3:7-8

Surely the Lord GOD does nothing, unless He reveals His secret to His servants the prophets. A lion has roared! Who will not fear? The Lord GOD has spoken! Who can but prophesy?

It has always been in God's plan to work with His servants, the prophets. Amos says(inv. 7) that God does nothing without revealing "His secret to his servants the prophets". Verse 8 continues, "The Lord GOD has spoken! Who can but prophesy?" When God speaks, a *prophet* listens, and he releases in total submission exactly what God has said.

Biblical Predictions by Prophets

Major changes and happenings in Israel's history were preceded by revelations from God through the prophets. God seldom acted without first alerting His people through a prophet. In the past, God used the prophetic voice to warn Israel, to instruct them, to announce an important event that would occur, or to affirm certain events among others.

Here are some specific prophecies:

- *Ahijah* prophesied the schism or division of Israel to Solomon (1 Kgs 11:31-19).
- The Bible speaks of an anonymous prophetic forecast that predicted Josiah's reform (1 Kgs 13:2-3).
- *Ahijah* predicted the death of Abijah and the end of the dynasty of Jeroboam (1 Kgs 14:6-16).
- *Elijah* prophesied the deaths of Ahab and Jezebel, as well as the extermination of Ahab's descendants (1 Kgs 21:17-19).
- *Elijah* also predicted the death of Ahaziah (2 Kgs 1:2-17).
- *Elisha* forecast Moab's defeat by Jehoram and Jehoshaphat (2 Kings 3).
- Micaiah predicted the fall of Ahab (1 Kings 22).
- Jeroboam II regained the lost Israelite territory in fulfilment of an unrecorded prophecy by *Jonah* (22 Kings 14:23–25).
- *Isaiah* predicted the invasion of Jerusalem by the Assyrians (Isa 10:5-15) and the extension of Hezekiah's life (Isaiah 38; 2 Kgs 20:6).
- Judah's exile to Babylon was repeatedly foretold to Hezekiah by Isaiah (2 Kgs 20:16) and to Manasseh by anonymous prophets (2 Kgs 21:10).
- King Josiah received prophecies of warning and counsel from *Huldah*, the prophetess (2 Kings 22).

- *Isaiah* predicted that Cyrus would lead the captives home from Babylon (Isa 45:1-5).
- *Isaiah* again predicted with accuracy the birth (Isa 7:14) and the death of our Lord Jesus Christ (Isa 53:5) centuries before it happened.
- *Jeremiah* predicted the captivity of Israel to Babylon, and that happened as he predicted (Jeremiah 25).

Here are some prophecies from the New Testament:

- The prophet *Agabus*, using a belt, accurately prophesied the arrest of Apostle Paul in Jerusalem (Acts 21:10-12).
- *Agabus* also prophesied that there would be a worldwide famine, and it is reported to have happened in the days of Claudius Caesar (Acts 11:28).
- *Paul* announced prophetically the Second Coming of our Lord Jesus Christ (2 Thessalonians 2).
- In a rapture, *John* in the Book of Revelation prophetically announced the end-time as it was revealed to him in graphic detail. He spoke about the heavens, the two witnesses (Rev 11:1-14), the binding of Satan for one thousand years, the war of Armageddon, and the Final Judgment (Revelation 20).

The Lord has always revealed His plans in advance to and through His servants, the prophets. The predictions could precede the events by years or even centuries, but the fulfilment was always certain. Since the Lord had now roared His judgment like a lion, who could but fear the outcome? God revealed His intentions to Amos, as the Scriptures declare (Amos 3:7): "Surely the Lord GOD does nothing, unless He reveals His secret to His servants the prophets". What then can the prophets do but prophesy God's message? If this is the pattern that God has used in ancient times with Amos and the other prophets, then it is important for us to heed the message echoed by King Solomon.

> ### Eccl 1:9-10
>
> That which has been is what will be, that which is done is what will be done, and there is nothing new under the sun. Is there anything of which it may be said, "See, this is new?" It has already been in ancient times before us.

History always repeats itself and God's promises are always reliable. This observation is true in the context of the Bible for otherwise the Old Testament would have become redundant and irrelevant to our faith today. The foundation of our doctrine in Christ is evident in the Old Testament, and everything that we enjoy in God has already had its manifestation, in different ways, in the days of old, either as a symbol, a prophetic utterance, or as an established track for us to follow. The message of the prophet Amos should not be taken lightly, just because it occurs in the Old Testament. All secrets are revealed to the servants of God, the prophets.

Some Prophecies in the Scriptures

- 1 Kings 11:29-39; fulfilled in 1 Kings 12:15-20
- 1 Kings 13:1-2; fulfilled in 2 Kings 23:15-20
- 1 Kings 14:1-16; fulfilled in 1 Kings 14:17-18; 15:29
- 1 Kings 21:17-24; fulfilled in 1 Kings 22:29-37; 2 Kings 9:30-10:11
- 2 Kings 1:2-4,16; fulfilled in 2 Kings 1:17
- 2 Kings 19:5-7, 20, 32-34; fulfilled in 2 Kings 19:35-37
- Isaiah 44:28; fulfilled in Ezra 1

CHAPTER ONE

THE PROPHETIC VOICE
BEFORE THE LAW

Contrary to popular thinking, the prophetic voice did not start with Moses. The sister of Moses, Miriam, is called a prophet (Ex 15:20). She leads a song and dance of victory, proclaiming the mighty things of God, during the exodus at the Reed Sea. Though Miriam is a prophetess, prophecy in fact started long before Moses and Miriam were even born.

There are two important figures, of great antiquity, who are described as prophets in the New Testament. Let's try to explore these related scriptures to understand them in the context of the prophetic voice. These two people are *Enoch* and *Noah*, both prophetic voices of their generation. God used both Enoch and Noah as prophets for His people. Those who carefully study the Bible attest that a strong and special anointing rested on these two biblical characters.

A question that can be asked with regard to the prophetic ministry of Enoch and Noah is: *How well did people in their time understand and accept their respective ministries?* If the Scriptures prove that they were misunderstood in their time, it would shed a bit of light on the misunderstanding that we face in our own generation regarding prophecy. We might realise that the problem of the prophetic, and how prophecy is perceived, started a long time ago. So far this point is an assumption, not a definite conclusion, until we interact with the Scriptures, for the Scriptures must be the final authority on all matters pertaining to life – including the matter of the prophetic voice.

Enoch

GEN 5:21-22

Enoch lived sixty-five years, and begot Methuselah. After he begot Methuselah, Enoch walked with God three hundred years, and had sons and daughters.

HEB 11:5

By faith Enoch was taken away so that he did not see death, "and was not found, because God had taken him"; for before he was taken he had this testimony, that he pleased God.

JUDE 1:14

Now *Enoch*, the seventh from Adam, *prophesied about these men* also, saying, "Behold, the Lord comes with ten thousands of His saints".

Enoch is the "seventh from Adam," says Jude. Seven is a sacred number. Freedom from death for Enoch is combined with this sacred number. Just as every seventh object was highly valued, so was the person of the seventh generation after Adam. Jude thus shows the antiquity and sacred character of Enoch's prophecies. There were only five fathers between Enoch and Adam, meaning that Enoch was the seventh father from Adam. The seventh from Adam, Enoch, prophesied the things that shall close the Seventh Age of the world. The reference of his prophecies was not to the antediluvians alone, but to all the ungodly. Enoch's prophecies indeed applied primarily to ancient times before the flood, but ultimately they looked ahead, also, to the Final Judgment.

From what we read in Jude, we understand that this letter confirms the pattern of God in dealing with His people throughout the ages. God always uses *a prophetic voice* to announce changes that need to take place in an era and a generation. In Jude 1, Enoch is surely confirmed as one who could prophesy, meaning that he had the ability to hear and to speak on behalf of God, and that is because he was indeed a prophet of God in his time. We shall speak more about Enoch below.

The Rise of the Prophetic Today

The rise of the prophetic voice in this era is an indication that there are major events and changes that are about to take place. For this reason God has now awakened the prophetic and raised its voice to establish and to accomplish His plan for this era.

If the church is not aligned with the prophetic, then it is headed for a shock. Without the might of the prophetic voice, the church will soon become directionless and irrelevant to our society. Already it is evident that the church is increasingly becoming a mere platform for moral support, motivational speeches, behavioural redirection and cultural affirmation, rather than being a place for spiritual happenings, a house of the supernatural, a refuge of hope and solutions, and a dwelling place of God.

An alarming number of people in our generation are losing interest in our faith, our doctrine and our God. Countries that were remarkably renowned in former times as model nations for Christ are completely secular today and make a deliberate effort to distance themselves from anything that is linked to the faith (namely, *Christianity*). Europe, which once sent missionaries throughout the world, is now largely indifferent when it comes to the faith. In the USA, the flames of God, kept burning for years, are now steadily being extinguished.

South Korea, which was a place of encounter and received millions upon its mountain of prayer, is becoming less and less noticeable on the Christian map.

Our young people are shying away from the church. Governments do not recognise our rightful place in society. We have almost no voice as the church today. The church has become so irrelevant that we are no longer part of the solution in society, but instead part of the problem. We speak of a great God but live in dismal mediocrity; those in society who choose a different route to ours seem to be better off than we are. We have nothing good to show for our faith.

We have become weak, laid-back and passive as the church. Our thirst for the glory of God has slackened. Our messages encourage passivity and lead our congregation to accept every calamity that may befall them as if fated and inevitable. Now, the church says, "If you are sick, maybe God is trying to teach you something through this disease. Be patient. Allow God to have His way for He knows best." If you are broke, we say, "Poverty is not that bad as long as you have the peace of God in you". If there is no progress in your life, the church says, "It is OK. If you achieve nothing in this world, you will achieve more in heaven."

Where is the church that challenges men and women to believe in God and to see His glory manifested in their day-to-day lives? Where is the church that leads people in prayer to God? This God said, "Call on Me and I will answer you. I will show you great things which you do not know" (Jer. 33:3). Where is the church of *Smith Wigglesworth, John Alexander Dowie, John Knox, Charles Grandison Finney, John Coe, John G. Lake, Lester Sumrall, Sadhu Sundar Singh, Kathryn Kuhlman, Maria Atta, A. A. Allen, William Marrion Branham, T. L. Osborn, Oral Roberts, Robert W. Schambach,* and *Benson Idahosa*, to name a few?

The future of the church looks so fuzzy in its current state that it is terrifying to imagine. I get goosebumps when I try to think of what the church will become twenty-five years from now! The remaining number of those who are still being used by God today will either have left to be with the Lord in glory or they will be in full retirement. Who will take over and run with the torch of the gospel of our Lord Jesus Christ? I truly believe that this renewal of the prophetic is a major reason why God is raising the prophetic voice in our own time.

Miracles and Technology

The world seems to believe in miracles more than the church does. As a result, in the secular realm, barriers of impossibilities are increasingly breaking through the current explosion in technology. The world is trying to achieve what the church, with all its proclamations, has failed to achieve. While the church is in slumber, the world is awakening to perform miracles for itself, to the point that it is becoming difficult for people to believe and follow our God since we *represent God so badly and introduce the supernatural so weakly.*

While we think that to prophesy is merely magic, the world is developing its technology to shape our future modes of communication. These modes have the appearance of permitting supernatural feats of communication or prophetic telepathy. The rise of the technological revolution with its *cloning and telepathic communication* will exclude communication gadgets; people will use mind-to-mind communication. It may seem impossible, like a simple fiction now, but these apparent miracles are bound to become our reality in the future. When these technological miracles become a reality, what will the church tell itself? That this is all magic?

The medical world is so advanced today that, whenever people are sick, the first thing that crosses their minds is the doctor not God, the healer (*Jehovah Rapha*). In the past, though people consulted their doctors freely, they knew that it was futile to expect health unless they had first turned to God for their healing. Today, this is not the case – not only for those who do not know God but also for those who belong to the church.

There is almost no supernatural healing taking place in our churches any longer, nor in the lives of believers. We have shut out the power of God so that it has become rare to experience its manifestation in our midst. We comfort ourselves with the obvious occurrence of natural events in our lives as if they were supernatural demonstrations of God's power. If you feel better from a headache, which you had due to the fact that you spent the day in the sun, you are not experiencing a supernatural demonstration of the power of God. The cure of the headache is an obvious and natural result.

Today, the fate of both believers and unbelievers is tied together. In fact, in many cases it seems like the unbeliever is better off than the believer, yet still there is no outcry amongst the believers. Why do the believers not cry to their God to show His presence? Where is the church that locks itself in prayer and fasting to seek the manifestation of the glory of God in its midst?

In Psalm 115, David cried out to the Lord:

> ### Ps 115:1-2
>
> Not unto us, O LORD, not unto us, but to Your name give glory, because of Your mercy, because of Your truth. Why should the nations say, "So where *is* their God?"

What are the churches doing besides fighting one another and trying to prove whose interpretation or version of the Scriptures is true? For those with heart problems, the medical world is able successfully to transplant a heart from one person to another. The same can be done with kidneys and other vital organs. The world is conducting medical trials in order to transplant heads from one person to another, with the expectation that the second person would use the new head (from the first person) as successfully as his own. These medical feats are neither magic nor tricks – they are the results of technology.

If the world believes it can successfully transplant a head, why would the church not trust in God to perform a simple miracle today? Should we really attribute miracles by God to demonic powers or believe that the servant of God stages them? I truly wonder if we still believe that our God is the God that the Bible proclaims. If we believed what the Scriptures say about our God, we would not struggle to attribute to Him every miracle in our lives. Our struggle would be in forsaking the belief that everything miraculous that we see comes from the Devil and his acolytes.

Cloning technology, which I mentioned earlier, may greatly bewilder many faith-based communities and be disruptive to many belief systems around the world. According to a news report, an American biotechnology company in Massachusetts, Advanced Cell Technology, made the world's first human clone of an adult.* As reported in 1998, they took a cell from Dr. Jose Cibelli, a research scientist, and combined it with a cow's egg from which the genes had already been removed. When the genes were activated, the egg started to divide normally, up to cell stage number 32, whereupon it was then destroyed. If the clone had been allowed to continue, it would have become Cibelli's identical twin. Technically, *1% of the*

* Patrick Dixon, "Cow / Human Clone Hybrid – Cow And Human Mixed Together," (unknown date): https://www. globalchange. com/humancow. htm

human clone genes would belong to the cow, namely the mitochondria genes. Mitochondria are power generators in the cytoplasm of the cell. They grow and divide inside cells and are passed on from one generation to the next. They are present insperm and eggs. Judging by the successful growth of the combined human-cow clone creation, it appears that cow mitochondria could be compatible with human embryonic development.

However, the biggest piece of news is not what scientists have done in human cloning – although this feat was sensational – but the fact that they kept cloning secret for three years after doing it; presumably they had been trying to perform cloning a couple of years before that, and they will continue doing so, whether openly or in secret.

For argument's sake, let's suppose that one day a cow, through cloning technology, should give birth to a human being. Would people still believe that human beings are created by God or even that our creation story is true? Would it be true that God created man in His image? *Or are people going to start thinking that it is man who created God in his imagination?* Unless we can bring fire down from heaven through an indisputable demonstration of the power of the Holy Ghost, which can stop the confusion, the church will be powerless to continue and prove its arguments.

The Body of Christ is currently so cold, and so unconcerned about the implications of its passivity and narrow-mindedness, that it couldn't care less if the entire world should be lost or not. The Church's attitude, in facing technology and the current challenges of faithlessness, is (I paraphrase), "Let them believe what they want to believe but we know the truth. God is greater than all". It may be the absolute truth that God is greater than all, but our current failure to demonstrate His power on earth gives the enemy an effortless opportunity to deceive many.

With love in our hearts, we need to witness demonstrations of the undiluted power of God to establish the kingdom on earth. In this way, we may empty Hell and fill up Heaven. The prophetic voice is here to play an important role in guiding the church and sustaining it amidst the many challenges ahead, including the challenges posed by all the current scientific accomplishments and the complexities of our day.

Sometimes, words alone are not enough to counter the onslaught of scientific accomplishments upon the church. We need something tangible and, as things stand now, the prophetic voice is to be the channel through which God will assert His authority. Seven generations after the creation, God chose a prophetic voice to announce major changes to come, and they happened as predicted and are still happening. Since we know that God does not change, we may expect that as He did in the past, so He is doing now and will do in the future. Is He not going to use the same means, the prophetic voice, to reveal His glory in our times?

The word *prophecy* (verb: *prophesy*) means literally, "to speak on behalf of or for," while it normally indicates *prediction, foretelling,* or *saying beforehand that something will happen.* Prophecies can be literal or symbolic. You cannot prophesy by a simple reliance on your instinct or your strong intuition. You need to be led by the Holy Spirit. A prophecy is not a sermon. So it cannot be prepared as one prepares a sermon. Prophecy is spiritual and manifests itself through revelation *only.*

The prophet must be attuned spiritually to God in order rightly to interpret and deliver the prophecy. Enoch is the model of such a prophet.

Who is Enoch?

Enoch comes from the prehistoric period in the Old Testament (i.e. the Hebrew Bible). He was a son of Jared and he fathered Methuselah. This Enoch is not to be confused with Cain's son Enoch in Gen 4:17.

GEN 5:21-24

Enoch lived sixty-five years, and begot Methuselah. After he begot Methuselah, Enoch walked with God three hundred years, and had sons and daughters. So all the days of Enoch were three hundred and sixty-five years. And Enoch walked with God; and he *was* not, for God took him.

The text of Genesis says that Enoch lived 365 years. The text reads that Enoch walked with God and then he was no more, for God took him. Some Christians interpret this scripture to mean that Enoch entered Heaven alive by an ascension, rapture or translation.

Enoch is the subject of many Jewish and Christian traditions. He was considered the author of the apocryphal Book of Enoch. He was also called "Enoch the scribe of judgment" based on references found in 1 Enoch 12:3-4, 15:1, and 92:1. The Christian New Testament has three references to Enoch.

LUKE 3:37

the *son* of Methuselah, *the son* of Enoch, *the son* of Jared, *the son* of Mahalalel, *the son* of Cainan.

> ### HEB 11:5
>
> By faith Enoch was taken away so that he did not see death, "and was not found, because God had taken him"; for before he was taken he had this testimony, that he pleased God.

> ### JUDE 1:14-15
>
> Now Enoch, the seventh from Adam, prophesied about these men also, saying, "Behold, the Lord comes with ten thousands of His saints, to execute judgment on all, to convict all who are ungodly among them of all their ungodly deeds which they have committed in an ungodly way, and of all the harsh things which ungodly sinners have spoken against Him".

Enoch appears in the book of Genesis as the seventh of the ten pre-flood patriarchs. Genesis recounts that each of the pre-flood patriarchs lived forseveral centuries. Genesis 5 provides a genealogy of these ten figures from Adam to Noah, providing the age at which each fathered the next child and the age of each figure at death.

Enoch is considered by many to be the exception, who is said *not* to have seen death (Heb 11:5).

Furthermore, Gen 5:22-29 states that Enoch lived 365 years, which is an extremely short life compared to that of his peers, who are all recorded as dying at over 700 years of age. The brief account of Enoch in Genesis 5 ends with the cryptic note that "he *was* not, for God took him" (v. 24).

This prophet Enoch is spoken of not only by Christians but also in classical rabbinical literature, which expresses a different view of him. One view regarding Enoch is found in Targum Pseudo- Jonathan, which thought of Enoch as a pious man, taken to heaven, who received the title of *Safra Rabba*, meaning *great scribe*.* After Christianity was completely separated from Judaism, this view became the prevailing rabbinical idea of Enoch's character and exaltation.

According to Rashi, (*Commentary on Gen 5:24*), commenting on Enoch,

> He was a righteous man, but his mind was easily induced to turn from his righteous ways and to become wicked. The Holy One, blessed be He, therefore took him away quickly and made him die before his full time. This is why Scripture uses a different expression when referring to his death by writing "and he was not", meaning, he was not in the world to complete the number of his years.†

In 3 Enoch (also called the *Sefer Hekhalot*), Rabbi Ishmael visits the Seventh Heaven where he meets Enoch. In 3 Enoch it is claimed that the earth had, in this time, been corrupted by the demons Shammazai and Azazel. Enoch is taken to Heaven and transformed into an angel and saved from corruption, to prove that God is merciful and not cruel.‡

Early Christianity contains various traditions concerning the translation of Enoch with regard to the quotation in Jude. Most early Christians considered that the traditions about Enoch did pre-date the flood. Regarding the Book of Enoch itself, Origen, Jerome, Augustine of Hippo, and all the church fathers mention

---

* For an overview, see Emil G. Hirsch and Solomon Schechter, "Enoch," *Jewish Encyclopedia* (1906 edition): http://www. jewishencyclopedia. com/ articles/5772-enoch

† Rashi, *Commentary on Genesis*, see: https://www. sefaria. org/Rashi_on_ Genesis? lang=bi

‡ 3 Enoch can be found here: https://archive. org/stream/ HebrewBook OfEnochenoch3/BookOfEnoch3_djvu. txt

this book. Justin Martyr, Athenagoras of Athens, Irenaeus, Clement of Alexandria, Lactantius, and others borrowed opinions from the book of Enoch. Tertullian, in several places, speaks of this book and argues that Noah preserved it during the flood.

In modern Christianity, Enoch is not counted as a saint in the Roman Catholic tradition, although Enoch has a saint's day, July 26, in the Armenian Apostolic church. Enoch is revered in the Tewahedo churches of the Ethiopian Orthodox Church, and the texts of Jubilees and Enoch are regarded as the 13th and 14th books, respectively, of the Tewahedo Old Testament canon.* Most churches, including the Catholic and the Greek Orthodox, do not accept these books. Protestants follow this Catholic view. Some church fathers, like John of Damascus, consider Enoch to be one of the two witnesses, mentioned in the Book of Revelation (Rev 11:3) as having come back to life, due to the fact that Enoch did not die (according to Gen 5:24). Some modern evangelical commentators also adhere to this view.

The Qur'an contains two references to Enoch.† In Surah Al-Anbiya, the so-called Prophet's verse, and in Surah Maryam, the so-called verses of Mary:

Q AL-ANBIYA 21:85

And Ishmael, and Enoch, and Ezekiel; each was one of the steadfast.

Q MARYAM 19:56-57

And mention in the Scripture Enoch. He was a man of truth, a prophet. And We raised him to a high position.

---

* See: https://www. ethiopianorthodox. org/english/canonical/books. html
† The citations from the Qur'an are based on this translation: https://www. clearquran. com/021. html and https://www. clearquran. com/019. html

Enoch is closely linked in Muslim tradition with the origins of writing and other technical arts of civilisation, including the study of astronomical phenomena. Enoch is credited with these arts, also, in the Jewish Testament of Abraham. Many Muslims honour Enoch as one of the earliest prophets.

Enoch: A Servant of God

As indicated by the evidence of different ancient literature, Enoch was certainly a prophet of the Lord and walked with God in his time in an amazing way.

If the Scriptures are taken at face value, we can conclude that God, when managing the affairs of this planet, always reveals His plan to his servant, the prophet, and the prophetic voice is an integral part of God's programme.

It is obviously not an exaggeration to declare that current theology seems to have deviated from the thinking of the prophet Amos. The notion expressed here is intrinsically rooted in biblical concepts of prophecy. The prophet stands in the presence of God. As Amos says, *the prophet is privy to the divine council* and, as the spokesman for the deity, the prophet is apprised in advance of God's plans.

The institution of prophecy is founded on the basic principle that God makes His will known to chosen individuals, as is clearly stated in Genesis. Jehovah reveals things to the prophet, which the prophet speaks or predicts. Jehovah makes known to the prophet the source of a prophecy. Then what the prophet predicts is really impending as Jehovah declares, and it will come to pass. Therefore, a prophecy is a foretelling, a voucher.

The divine origins of prophecy are from God himself. Calling a prophet a "servant of God" (e.g. Isa 49:5) is a standard Old Testament theme. This theme occurs frequently in other prophetic and historical writings. Just as a king has high-ranking officers in his service, so the Lord has His officers, the prophets. In this context, it is the status of the prophet, not the act of serving, that is emphasised.

Where languages have distinctive terms for "servant" according to what they do or their social position, it may be easy to select an appropriate equivalent term. In other languages without such exact terminology, it is necessary to translate the term "servant" when referring to a prophet as "one who works for Him" or "helper". The servant of God, who speaks for God: that is what the prophetic voice is all about.

To understand the special role and call of the prophet, who takes counsel from the Lord, consider these scriptures: Jeremiah 15, Isaiah 6, Jer. 23:18, 22, and Gen. 18:17 (Abraham is called a prophet in Gen 20:7).

About Noah

GEN 6:9

This is the genealogy of Noah. Noah was a just man, perfect in his generations. Noah walked with God.

2 PET 2:5

And did not spare the ancient world, but saved Noah, *one of* eight *people*, a preacher of righteousness, bringing in the flood on the world of the ungodly.

God spoke directly to Noah as he did to Adam before him and many prophets after him. Noah was God's spokesperson and representative. As Peter explains, Noah was a preacher of righteousness, who foretold the flood to his contemporaries, warning them of the coming judgement.

Noah was able to hear God and prophetically speak His word and announce His plans to His people Israel, predicting literally and accurately what was to come. He operated as a prehistoric prophet in his time.

In turn, God provided Noah with a sign of a new covenant after the flood. Through a rainbow, God signalled His promise of peace through Noah and to the coming generations. In this way, too, God shared His counsel with Noah, his righteous servant.

GEN 9:12-17

And God said: "This *is* the sign of the covenant which I make between Me and you, and every living creature that *is* with you, for perpetual generations: I set My rainbow in the cloud, and it shall be for the sign of the covenant between Me and the earth. It shall be, when I bring a cloud over the earth, that the rainbow shall be seen in the cloud; and I will remember My covenant which is between Me and you and every living creature of all flesh; the waters shall never again become a flood to destroy all flesh. The rainbow shall be in the cloud, and I will look on it to remember the everlasting covenant between God and every living creature of all flesh that *is* on the earth." And God said to Noah, "This *is* the sign of the covenant which I have established between Me and all flesh that is on the earth".

CHAPTER TWO

THE INSTITUTION OF THE
PROPHETIC VOICE

Ex 20:18-19

Now all the people witnessed the thunderings, the lightning flashes, the sound of the trumpet, and the mountain smoking; and when the people saw *it*, they trembled and stood afar off. Then they said to Moses, "You speak with us, and we will hear; but let not God speak with us, lest we die".

In this biblical scene, the people of Israel witness something splendid upon Mt Sinai: a manifestation of the power of God (called a theophany), by thunder, lightening, smoke and the sound of a trumpet. This spectacle, during the time of Moses, officially inaugurates the prophetic voice as we still have it today.

Throughout the book of Exodus in the Bible, a group of people, who have been slaves for about 430 years in Egypt, hold onto great promises from God: promises of freedom, prosperity, fruitfulness, and the multiplication of good things. These enslaved people are subjected to all kinds of exploitation and atrocities at the hand of the Egyptians until, at last, God raises up Moses to set them free. Through a strong demonstration of the power of God, of the kind also visible to Israel upon Mt Sinai, Pharaoh and the whole of Egypt are finally brought to their knees. The Egyptian overlords release the children of Israel from their land.

In the verses above, depicting a theophany on the mountain top, God addresses the people directly while in the process of building Israel into a nation. Yahweh wants to reveal Himself to them so that they may know that they are different from all other nations on the face of the earth, for they are God's people.

Babel and the Making of Israel as God's People

Before going through the theophany from Exodus 20 in depth, allow me to take you through another portion of Scripture that explains God's choice to build a new nation of His own people. Many people have not quite paid attention to this act of God, which is so significant in the history and nation of Israel.

> ### DEUT 32:8-9
>
> When the Most High divided their inheritance to the nations, When He separated the sons of Adam, He set the boundaries of the peoples According to the number of the children of Israel. For the Lord's portion *is His people;* Jacob *is the place of His inheritance.*

In *Supernatural: What the Bible Teaches About the Unseen World – and Why It Matters,* the American biblical scholar Michael Heiser explains these verses with clarity.*[15] When God divided up the nations, they were divided among the sons of God. God allotted the nations to members of His divine council. This form of government is the Bible's explanation for why other nations came to worship other gods. Until Babel, God wanted a relationship with all humanity. But the rebellion at Babel changed that. So, God decided to create a new nation, called His "portion", which in Deut 32:9 means Israel. This

---

* Heiser, ch. 13.

new nation begins with the call of Abraham in Genesis 12, the very next chapter after the Tower of Babel.

From this point onward, the Old Testament recounts how the God of Israel and His people, the Israelites, are in conflict with the gods and the people of other nations. Even so, when God makes His covenant with Abraham, He makes it clear that "in you all the families of the earth shall be blessed" (Gen 12:3). God had been planning, from the beginning, to bring the nations back into His family at some point and to heal the divisions and conflicts.

The scene in Genesis 11 tells about Babel, where the people of the world gather to worship from the top of a tall structure. When God says, "Let Us go down and there confuse their language" (Gen 11:7), we are reminded of what God says as Adam and Eve leave the Garden of Eden: "Behold, the man has become like one of Us" (Gen 3:22). In both cases, God sends the offending people out, away from where they have been living. These scenes introduce the idea of cosmic geography. God uses land and geography (i.e. physical space) to define borders and to designate inherited rights of ownership; even the dirt in the fields can tell the story of God's people and their ultimate salvation.

To claim His own portion, God chose and called Abraham so that through him He might create a nation that would be His and be called according to His name. The story of Abraham eventually finds fulfilment in the Messiah, the anointed one of God, who is Jesus Christ. All the smaller parts of the biblical story find their proper expression through the story of Abraham, his family and their relationship to God and the gods of other nations.

Mt Sinai

Having just reviewed some points about biblical salvation history, the question arises how this salvation history relates to the rise of the prophetic voice. In order to answer this question, we must return to the scene on Mt Sinai, where we started the chapter. As we will see, in this scene the people of Israel ask Moses to be a mediator and prophet, who speaks for God. The prophetic voice is inaugurated here, at this turning point in Israel's salvation history, when the people are to become a nation.

Recall that the story of Abraham is placed immediately after the worldwide flood and the subsequent apportionment of lands and peoples to the authority of created gods. The Psalmist recalls these combined incidents. "The Lord sat enthroned at the Flood" (Ps 20:10), delegating His leadership over creation by commanding within it the stewardship of gods. When Abraham is called by God to turn away from his worship of the god of the city of Ur, the story draws us in with fascinating possibilities.

His family, the nation of Israel, were slaves in Egypt for 430 years, but here, on this mountain of Sinai, they are about to become a nation and *something drastic is about to happen*. Yahweh, the creator of Heaven and Earth, the visible and the invisible God, is about *to show Himself to His beloved people, the Israelites*. The scene is terrifying; they have never experienced such a thing in their lives. Yes, the Israelites knew God and how powerful He was because of what they had seen in Egypt, and throughout their history up to this point. They knew God, but they had never experienced Him in the way that He now introduced Himself to them. To experience thunder, lightning and smoke on the mountain is just a preamble to a direct encounter. For fear of a real encounter with God in which they would hear the divine voice directly, the people beg Moses not to expose them to this magnificent yet ominous reality. They fear they will not be able to handle such an awesome meeting.

> ## Ex 20:19
>
> Then they said to Moses, "You speak with us, and we will hear; but let not God speak with us, lest we die".

They beg Moses to act as an intermediary and to play the role of God's mouthpiece for them. To Moses, they say that they fear they will die if they allow God to speak to them. Their reasoning seems to be like this (I paraphrase): "We cannot stand before this God; His glory is so overwhelming to us that we fear we might be crushed in His presence; now, if it is possible, you, Moses, must speak to God and let us hear from you and not from God directly."

For me, this request by the people is a turning point in the history of the people of Israel. In essence, they are telling Moses to be the *prophetic voice of God*, to hear for them and to make the divine known on their behalf.

Since to hear God speak audibly was frightening for the Israelites, they asked for the *prophetic* to assist, and that Moses should be that prophetic voice, who would always relay God's words to them reliably. This request makes considerable sense in the light of the consistent biblical witness to the ear-shattering volume of the voice of God. In all other cases where God is recorded as speaking audibly, the sound is described as deafeningly loud (Ezek 43:2).

Moses was somehow able to endure God's voice, presumably by special divine grace, but average Israelites found this possibility so terrifying that they wanted nothing more of it. It was not merely the sound of God's words, of course, that had such a frightening effect; the people saw the *thunder* and *lightning*, heard *the trumpet* and saw the *mountain in smoke*, and that combination of sensory data, along with the voice of God, would be way too much for them. So, they trembled with fear and stayed at a distance.

This holding back was no mere choice of convenience for the people. They perceived that they could not repeatedly endure having to hear God speak directly to them. As an alternative, Moses therefore approached God directly, but the people stood far away. It is important to understand that there is a dimension of the presence of God that is somehow threatening even to His own people; we need grace to be able to handle this tremendous thing.

The fear of dying that the Israelites voiced to Moses may have come from the idea that nearness to God would result in death, as already announced in the preceding verses (Ex 19:21). Then, hearing the voice of God as if He were shouting in one's eardrum might suggest a similar sort of potentially fatal proximity.

The fear of Yahweh gripped them; they could never again take Him or His words lightly. His presence was so overwhelming that they asked Moses to be their intermediary at Sinai and to establish the conditions of their covenant. All along, this was Yahweh's plan so that trust in Moses might be established. That goal would be fulfilled. In Ex 20:19, the thought is as follows: "You yourself speak with us and we will indeed pay attention". The Hebrew indicates an emphatic construction that drives home the recognition of Moses' authority over the people and their recognition of this authority; he would be their intermediary.

Though I believe that we as *born again* have received a new lease on life in Him that allows us the ability to stand in the presence of God, and that we have Jesus Christ as our sole mediator, it is important to note that the above text is the official birth of the prophetic in the kingdom of God. The prophetic, born long ago on Mt Sinai, continues in the form that we see and experience it today.

No prophet in modern times is appointed to be a *mediator* of any sort between men and God, but prophets are in our time anointed to be facilitators of God's will. It is to be noted that there is an aspect in the prophetic of old that was mainly meant for those who lived under the Old Covenant. This aspect of prophecy is no longer relevant to us since, on the Cross of Calvary when Jesus died, the veil was torn. Prophecy of the Old Testament kind is changed and also *fulfilled* by the rending of the Temple veil. In the time of Moses, Israel had no other means to communicate and hear directly from God except through Moses, His prophet. However now, though we have prophets, every child of God may freely communicate with God and hear from Him.

Do We Still Need Prophets in Our Time?

This question may arise for many of us. We do still need prophets in our time and in our lives for a number of reasons, which I will discuss here.

1. Prophecy, and the office of the prophet, are established by the will of God

The office of the prophet is established by the Lord our God Himself. Prophets are not aliens that have come to invade our planet illegally; they are men and women carefully selected by God and called to serve Him just as the rest of His servants do, who operate in various other fields of the ministry. So, it is imperative that we always remember that prophets, according to the Scriptures, are established by the will of God in our lives.

The Body of Christ cannot do without prophets; the Body of Christ will not reach its desired perfection without the prophetic ministry, which ought to be playing its role fully. Prophets are not improvisational fellows who come to disturb the harmony of the church by their strange, unconventional and off-key operations. They come about as the result of the perfect and sovereign will of God for the church. Their cutting-edge ministry is indispensable for the church, especially in times such as these, our own times.

Though a prophet is not a mediator between us and God, he or she remains an expert communicator used by God to convey special messages to us.

As children of God, we have all been given access to the Father. We can speak to Him directly, we can hear Him also. His word is made available to us, His children, and we can understand it. While all this is true, God understands that, as His children, we need help to fully mature to the potential He has in mind for us. Thus, in His great love for us, Jesus has given us gifts (*the five-fold ministry*) for the perfection of the saints.

Though we can pray ourselves, prophets are people appointed by God to help us in prayer and to teach us how to pray; they pray with us and pray for us. The same is true with the Word. Although the Scriptures are widely available to us, Christ gave us His servants to help us access these Scriptures; they read the Word with us and for us, they build our faith in the Word, and they teach us to observe all that is written. And though we can speak to God and hear Him also, our Lord knew that communication is a process that requires someone of a special anointing to assist us. Thus, He raised men and women, whom He selected and anointed as prophets, and endowed with spiritual abilities. They operate in the spiritual realm so that they may speak His words to us and guide us.

Look at it this way. When you are sick, although you can self-administer medication bought from a pharmacy (it is your right), self-medication might not be enough to heal you. Thus, society has trained people with specific skills in health to assist you when you are sick. This does not mean that you can no longer take your own medication to relieve mild pain, but you are advised to consult professionals for anything serious.

Similarly, in the spiritual realm regarding the prophetic, although we can hear God ourselves, He has anointed and equipped some people differently to assist us in our quest to communicate with Him. Their presence does not imply that our right to speak to God has been abolished; on the contrary, it has been affirmed. The prophet is established in the church to help us as children of God; the prophet is not our way to the Father for only Jesus is the way to the Father.

2. A prophet is God's servant sent to guide us

The prophet possesses certain abilities generally not given to all believers. The work of others is not limited to that of relaying what God is saying to His people; through the ability given to them to see into the future and into the invisible realm, prophets have better insight into things of the Spirit and can better guide God's people. In other words, the prophet not only says what he hears God say; by himself, through the vast treasure that the prophetic affords him, he also leads and guides the people of God according to what he sees in the invisible world and for the future.

For example, sometimes the prophet in your life may warn you of something, not because of some warning from God, but simply because, through his spiritual eyes, he is able to see danger ahead for you. Prophet Agabus, for instance, used the belt of Paul to indicate to him that he would be bound in Jerusalem. This prophet did not necessarily hear a command from God, warning Paul not to go to

Jerusalem, for if that were so Paul would not have gone to Jerusalem (lest he refuse God). Instead, the prophet foresaw Paul's arrest in the spiritual. Consequently, Paul had the choice of cancelling the trip or proceeding even though he knew that he would be arrested.

Prophetic Abilities

As a prophet, I have abilities that are indescribable. I literally see so much that I am left to believe sometimes that I see everything. By the grace of God, I am able, in a split second, to gain fifty years worth of information about people, down to the smallest details of their past, present and future. I can, at that moment, recognise their challenges and their cherished causes. I am in a better position, because of my prophetic knowledge, to guide them to success.

A prophet is not a journalist. What you hear or see in prophecy is not always to be announced, directly; rather, these messages should be conveyed quietly to guide people and stand by them in prayer. A prophet is able to see the cause of your pain in the spiritual realm and to lead you out of a lifetime of struggle – all in a moment. I always say, "You cannot be defeated if you have a true prophet guiding you". This is why every great king who ruled Israel had a prophet of God close to him. Through the counsel of the prophet, the king ruled God's people.

CHAPTER THREE

THE END OF THE PROPHETIC VOICE

Some believers advocate that the prophetic voice, and a number of other gifts of the Spirit seen in the Bible, are not for our times today. These gifts were good for yesterday, and for earlier times; they ceased to exist during the former times, in the days of the biblical prophets and the apostles. This position is known as *cessationism*, held by the *cessation school* or *the cessationists*.

The cessationists believe that supernatural gifts were reserved only for the biblical prophets and apostles and, since they are no longer alive, these gifts have ceased to exist for us. In simple language, they believe that when the biblical prophets and apostles died, they died and took away with them (so to speak) all the supernatural gifts of the Holy Spirit. For them, the gifts of the Holy Spirit were *one-off*.

Does the Bible Predict the End of the Prophetic?

The text to which they appeal is 1 Corinthians 13, to support their argument. But, does 1 Corinthians 13 really suggest the cessation of the supernatural gifts of the Holy Spirit or support their doctrine? It is important to allow this scripture to speak for itself.

1 Cor 13: 8-10

Love never fails. But whether *there are* prophecies, they will fail; whether *there are* tongues, they will cease; whether *there is* knowledge, it will vanish away. For we know in part and we prophesy in part. But when that which is perfect has come, then that which is in part will be done away.

Many schools of thought have developed on the basis of this passage. There is a template that each person possesses when it comes to analysing facts, and it is labelled a *filter*. A filter, in this sense, is used to eliminate things in order to achieve a desired result. For example, a filter in cooking eliminates unwanted elements from our meal; these elements are dredged, strained and discarded. When used in our cars, filters prevent particles from interfering with mechanical operations and performance. When used in an email, filters weed out messages that we don't want to read. Therefore what is left, after the contents have been filtered, are things that we may use: whatever contributes to our meal, our engine or our sanity.

The same applies to our interpretation of the Word of God. We use *mental filters* to adjust what the Scripture is saying to suit our preconceived needs or viewpoints. For example, we label verses that do not quite suit our wishes as "problem passages", and we either filter them out or label them as being of no importance; or worse, we give different interpretations to certain scriptures in order to suit our inclinations.

A lot of well-meaning biblical scholars, pastors and professors fall short of the intentional self-scrutiny required in order to maintain objectivity in consulting the Scriptures. Many scholars view the Bible through the lens of what they know and what is familiar to them. Therefore, their research may be mainly aimed at finding affirmations for their initial learning and doctrines.

The Rise of the Prophetic Voice

For example, if their first learning tells them that casting out demons is not a biblical practice, then their research of the Scriptures may confirm this bias without yielding other results. They will find stronger evidence to confirm for themselves, and their designated audience, their theories that exorcism (or casting out demons) is not biblical. Their minds are already programmed to think in a certain way; their minds will automatically sound an alert if any information challenges their accepted convictions. So, they will reject such information immediately, without pause or reflection.

Michael Heiser puts it this way: "Our traditions, however honourable, are not intrinsic to the Bible. They are systems we invent to organise the Bible. They are artificial. They are filters."*

The scripture 1 Cor 13:8-10 has been used by the cessation school to support the end of a prophetical voice. The cessationists have held that modern prophets are false prophets. An analysis of 1 Cor 13:8-10 raises the following questions. Does this passage really predict the end of the prophetic voice in our era? Do we have sufficient empirical evidence to arrive at this conclusion? Did we give ourselves enough time to allow for a proper interpretation of the Bible, or did we allow our traditions to once again influence our interpretation? Did we already label these so-called prophets as being lost so that now we try to justify our prejudices by forcing certain passages of the Scriptures to be discarded while we discredit others? All these questions necessitate a thorough investigation.

The main subject of 1 Cor 13:8-10 concerns the eschatological nature of spiritual gifts. Here, the concept of the *eschatological* (i.e. relating to the *end times*) bears particularly on the gifts of prophecies, tongues and knowledge. According to the passage, there will come a

---

* Heiser, ch. 2.

day (at the end or fulfilment of time) when such spiritual gifts will no longer be needed. Then, only love will remain.

> **1 Cor 13:8**
>
> Love never fails. But whether *there are prophecies* [emphasis added to "prophecies"] they will fail; whether *there are* tongues, they will cease; whether *there is* knowledge, it will vanish away.

Clearly, Paul is announcing the cessation of the prophetic along with other spiritual gifts, but the question we should ask ourselves is about the time reference. Was he announcing that the cessation would happen in our times today or rather at the end of time? I would think that many of those who lived in the time of Paul were also eager to understand whether he was referring to the cessation of the prophetic during their lives or at another time. The apostle Paul's statement relates purely to the end times (and to what we might call the rapture). He was referring to a future *eschatological* event associated with Christ's Second Coming. Scholars generally agree that the basic principle behind Paul's statement is that spiritual gifts serve a temporary function among believers until the end times and the last things.

The role of the prophetic, as we know it, is terrestrial or pertaining to the earth. Paul seems to refer here to a state of the church that will be established in heavenly glory (or after the rapture). At that time, there will be no further need for prophecies. Love will never fail, as the apostle Paul highlights in 1 Cor 13:8. Because God Himself is love, the ministry of love will continue even in Heaven. This fundamental truth pertains to all existing ministries. Gifts on earth may be characterised as *pastoral, evangelical* and *apostolic*. There are gifts of *teaching, healing, miracles, discernment of spirits* and so on. The assignment of these ministries and spiritual gifts is for the service of the Body of Christ, in particular, and the world, in general, while still on earth.

Since our church exists still on earth, so does prophecy exist, together with the other gifts of the Spirit.

A close look at 1 Cor 14:1-5, furthermore, introduces a fact that cannot be disputed. The apostle Paul, inspired by the Holy Spirit, wrote:

> Pursue love, and desire spiritual *gifts*, but especially that you may prophesy. For he who speaks in a tongue does not speak to men but to God, for no one understands *him*; however, in the spirit he speaks mysteries. But he who prophesies speaks edification and exhortation and comfort to men. He who speaks in a tongue edifies himself, but he who prophesies edifies the church. I wish you all spoke with tongues, but even more, that you prophesied; for he who prophesies is greater than he who speaks with tongues, unless indeed he interprets, that the church may receive edification.

In this text, let us emphasise the phrase *"especially that you may prophesy"* (v.1), which establishes the ranking of prophecy among the spiritual gifts. The concept of *prophecy* refers to utterances inspired by the Holy Spirit, and we see that the apostle Paul elevates the *prophetic gift* above the gift of tongues.

Like the Old Testament prophets, the prophets in the New Testament take on a role that involves social critique. The prophet calls the community to repentance and reveals God's future plans for both salvation and judgement. Such utterances may include predictions of the future that are intended to encourage or challenge believers, not to confuse them. In 1 Corinthians 11 and 14, prophets in the congregation prophesy and Paul must set down rules to curtail chaos. Prophetic speech ought to build up the church even though it can cause lively debates and disorder.

Paul's discussion contrasts the benefits of prophecy with tongues. Why would he have spoken about the end of the prophetic on earth in this passage, while in the very next chapter he exalts the role of prophecy in the church and the world? If the prophetic voice is present for the edification of the church (as mentioned by Paul), and given that the church is still present here on earth, it is completely confusing how one could conclude that the prophetic voice has ceased. If the prophet's role is to announce the mighty things of God, surely God's mighty revelations have not ceased. The logical conclusion is that the prophetic is in fact a reality for the church on earth.

According to Paul, speaking in tongues is for self-edification, but to prophesy is for the edification of others. Paul shows that the aim of authentic prophecy is to build up the whole community: to exhort, to comfort, to console and to encourage. Some commentators interpret 1 Cor 14:15 to mean that prophecy amounts to constructive and life-giving preaching, proclamations or teachings that are pastorally sensitive, applied in order to share the gospel of truth for helping others. While prophecy aims ultimately to build up the whole community, as Paul states, prophecy is more powerful – and usually more controversial – than this definition admits. The prophetic gift aims ultimately to build up the church, according to Paul. Yet, as we can tell in both the OT and the NT, more generally, prophecy can disturb people. Such misinterpretations are the result of the phenomenon of mental *filters* (discussed above), which are templates that shape our explanations.

E. P. Sanders argues that Paul understands his own commission to preach the apostolic gospel to the Gentiles in prophetic terms. It is widely agreed that Paul's commission reflects Jeremiah's call "from before birth" (Jer 1:4-5).* Sanders points out that in post-canonical Judaism, the term "prophet" denoted a wide range of leadership activities: the famous hymn in honour of leaders that begins "Let us now sing the praises of famous men" (Sir 44:1) includes Moses, Nathan, Elijah, Zerubbabel and others who, by their intelligible communicative actions, lead the people to give praise to God for his saving acts (Sirach 44-50). Paul himself, Sanders insists, stands in this prophetic tradition..

In conclusion, note that the prophetic ministry is an earthly ministry in the service of the church and the world. As long as the church and the Body of Christ remain on earth, the prophetic ministry will be in full operation. Prophecy will cease only after the church has been raptured in glory, because prophets, pastors, evangelists, teachers and apostles aren't needed in Heaven.

---

* E. P. Sanders, *Paul and Palestinian Judaism: 40th Anniversary Edition* (Minneapolis: Fortress Press, 2017).

CHAPTER FOUR

THE PROPHETIC ANOINTING, GIFT AND CALLING

The prophetic movement is great and vast, with different ways of operating. In this chapter, I will set forth three channels of expression for the prophetic in our times. This discussion is aimed mainly to help you to recognise yourself among the three prophetic roles. Every one of us with a prophetic vocation functions within one of these three spheres.

In the prophetic, some are prophets by calling, some are carriers of the prophetic gift, and the rest operate under a prophetic anointing. In this prophetic era, the entire Body of Christ is wrapped by a prophetic grace, irrespective of one's position and purpose in the kingdom. Even those who are not called to be in full-time ministry are called to be prophetic. To be prophetic is to be in the atmosphere of the prophetic and to flow in accordance with where the Spirit of God is leading you in this season. May the Spirit of God right now prompt you to locate your prophetic anchor, whether it be found in an *anointing*, or a *gift*, or a *calling*.

The Prophetic Anointing

Perhaps our first task is to define anointing. An anointing is a supernatural ability given to a person to fulfil a given task. Anointing indicates supernatural empowerment. When we speak of the anointing of the Holy Spirit, we refer to the supernatural empowerment that someone receives from the Holy Spirit of God for the assignment he has received from God to undertake on earth. The anointing is given proportionately to the assignment received. An anointing is never given for fame or show, but rather to fulfil a task, an assignment or a mission on earth for the glory of God.

Your assignment will determine your anointing. To receive the type of anointing belonging to another is only possible if you can first receive this person's assignment and share his burden. Elisha desired to continue and fulfil the mission of Elijah. He asked for double his anointing (2 Kgs 2:9). When Elijah warned him of the difficulties, for which he had petitioned, the elder holy man referred not to the anointing itself but rather to the assignment: "You have asked a hard thing. *Nevertheless,* **if you see me** *when I am* **taken from you, it shall be so for you; but if not, it shall not be** *so*" (2 Kgs 2:10).

Elijah meant that Elisha had to draw a boundary as to where Elijah's assignment stopped so that Elisha's might begin. The mantle that Elijah left behind (2 Kgs 2:13) represented both his assignment and the grace to fulfil it. If Elisha had not been with Elijah at the time of his rapture to Heaven, he would have missed his opportunity to take up his elder's mantle, which represents his assignment and anointing (2 Kgs 2:14).

Your anointing is conditional upon your assignment. So, although you can increase your anointing to fit the level of your assignment, your anointing level can never supersedeorexceedyour assignment. If you sense that your task is greater than the anointing you have for it, you may ask God to increase your anointing to match your assignment. If you should then want more anointing than what is required, you will have to ask God to give you a greater mission. With the extra responsibility, you may also receive a greater anointing.

Always remember that anointing is never for its own sake; anointing occurs for some purpose.

What is the prophetic anointing? The prophetic anointing is the ability that God gives to any of His children to operate in the prophetic. The anointing serves mainly to guide and build us by the will of God. This anointing primarily helps the one on whom it is bestowed; it is only in rare instances that it may work for someone else through him. Through anointing, you develop into a prophet over your own life, which enables you to think like a prophet and act like a prophet. You know the will of God in pressing matters of your life and navigate through difficult circumstances with prophetic insight and faith.

Here, the prophetic anointing empowers the children of God to operate in the prophetic even though they may not necessarily be recipients of the prophetic gift or calling (of which we will speak below). Children of God with a prophetic anointing may not even be in full-time ministry. Even so, they are open to being used by God in the prophetic.

In general, the anointing of God is possible for everyone who is given a task by the Lord in life. This includes those who are prophets by calling or who simply have a gift of prophecy. Please note that I am talking here specifically about the *prophetic anointing* and not merely about the general anointing of God, which helps all of us to operate and to succeed in our various tasks and forms of life.

Note that no one can operate in the prophetic by himself; we need a supernatural ability to do so. The prophetic does not rely on the natural realm, such as the mind or learned eloquence. In fact, the Bible recommends that we "examine prophecies and take only what is good" (1 Thess 5:20-21); when human will, mind and self enter into prophecy, the message is no longer pure but instead contaminated by the prophet's emotions, feelings and personal interpretations. God's entire message for His people may get corrupted or derailed by personal factors. You can only operate in the prophetic realm from a supernatural position, relying only on the supernatural ability of the Holy Spirit. This is not the case when it comes to other ministries.

You may not need supernatural power to preach a good sermon or to sing a beautiful Christian hymn. However, in the realm of the prophetic, it is impossible to operate without having been supernaturally empowered to do so. In the prophetic, your mind and academic qualifications will not help you; your life experience and your burning desire and intentions will also not help you; you are helped only by the anointing of the Holy Spirit upon your life for prophecy. The good news is that in this end of times the Spirit of the Lord has made available His anointing for every believer in the Body of Christ – in accord with prophecy of old (see Joel 2:28-29).

The prophetic anointing comes upon anyone who avails him or herself as a pliable instrument of the Lord. You do not need to be a full-time minister or a church leader to be prophetic. The prophetic anointing can be bestowed on various people in different walks of life: an infant, a child, the young, students, ordinary members of the community, employees, entrepreneurs, civil servants, officials, political leaders, and so forth.

When this anointing comes on you, you will have the spiritual ability to operate fully in the prophetic, proportionately to the level of your anointing. Please note that the prophetic anointing does not make you a prophet; it just gives you the ability to flow like one for a specific period of time and for a specific mission.

Here is a remarkable story from 1 Samuel 10 that may shed light on how the prophetic anointing functions. Saul was the first King of Israel. Samuel anointed him king when he went to him, looking

for the lost donkeys of his father. On his return, the Bible says
something happened to Samuel:

> ### 1 Sam 10:9-12
>
> So it was, when he had turned his back to go from Samuel, that God
> gave him another heart; and all those signs came to pass that day. **10**
> When they came there to the hill, there was a group of prophets to
> meet him; then the Spirit of God came upon him, and he prophesied
> among them. **11** And it happened, when all who knew him formerly
> saw that he indeed prophesied among the prophets, that the people
> said to one another, "What *is* **this** *that* **has come upon the son of
> Kish?** *Is* **Saul also among the prophets?**" **12** Then a man from there
> answered and said, "But who *is* **their father?**" Therefore it became
> a proverb: "*Is* **Saul also among the prophets?**"

In the scripture above, Saul, a young man who is set to become the
first king of Israel, suddenly begins prophesying when he meets a
group of prophets. He prophesies just like them, so much so that
those who have known him before wonder if he has also become a
prophet. Is Saul indeed becoming a prophet? No, Saul is anointed
to become the first king of Israel. He has never prophesied before
that day, and he is not a prophet. So then how is it that we see him
prophesying in this scripture? What happens is that, while in the
presence of a group of prophets, Saul, who is already very sensitive
in the Spirit after his earlier encounter with the prophet Samuel,
has been seized by the Holy Spirit; a prophetic anointing comes
upon him at that time, leading him to prophesy just as the other
prophets do.

Though Saul prophesied that day, he was never reported to prophesy
thereafter because he was not a prophet. The prophetic anointing
is not permanent upon a person; it comes upon you as and when it
needs to. This is how the prophetic anointing functions; it comes

upon you to help you to fulfil a prophetic task, even though you may not be called to be a prophet. I love this anointing because of its fewer restrictions; it is for every believer irrespective of whether or not they are called to be a prophet.

Is the Prophetic Anointing Permanent in a Person's Life?

Though a person can remain permanently in the prophetic realm, the prophetic anointing in his or her life has to be renewed regularly for it is not permanent. It is like manna that the children of Israel ate in the desert; they had to collect it every morning and could not keep it until the next day. They needed new manna each day (Ex 16:14-21). Many have had a miraculous experience once in their lives while being used prophetically by God. Yet they were never used again. It is not for a lack of spiritual assignments that people are no longer used by God for this anointing. Rather, they fail to avail themselves, continually, of the prophetic anointing of God in their lives. An engine that has run out of oil will not be able to function unless there is a refill; and operating such an engine without a refill might cause irreparable damages.

Eccl 9:8

Let your garments always be white, and let your head lack no oil.

This verse speaks of the anointing, which is abundant and never lacking.

What Can We Do to Flow in the Prophetic Anointing?

Allow me to underline for you that God is sovereign, and that in His sovereignty He can use anyone as He pleases. Yet, in God's goodness, God is not arbitrary or capricious. He makes use of us in ways that develop our capacities and fulfil our desires. In the context of the prophetic anointing, God's sovereignty often rules His interventions. Even Balaam's donkey prophesied. God can bring a prophetic anointing on anyone, in any circumstances, even without people's own efforts to draw the anointing into their lives.

With that said, there are things that we can do to draw the prophetic anointing to ourselves, and here I share with you five important steps to take: *believe, desire, avail yourself, pay the price* and *be in a prophetic environment.*

Believe

Belief is where prophetic anointing all begins. You won't get a prophetic anointing to manifest in your life simply to satisfy your curiosity. This is why spiritual enlightenment through teaching is crucial; it will help to shed light on the truth, and faith will be ignited in people's hearts. You must believe that such anointing exists in God for His children, and you must firmly believe that you are the right candidate for it. Unless there is such a belief in your heart, you will forfeit its presence in your life.

Refuse the lies of the Devil that such anointing cannot be bestowed on you by God. And also refuse to believe that you are too unholy or unqualified to be endowed by it. Open your heart to everything that God has in store for you today. Please say this simple prayer with me:

> Lord Jesus, I thank you for the Cross and for sending the Holy Spirit to us after your ascension to the Father. I open myself to the works of the Holy Spirit in my life and through my life. I believe that His anointing for the prophetic is my portion today and that I am a worthy vessel for it through the precious blood of Jesus Christ. Amen.

Desire

Your desires form a considerable force of attraction in the spiritual realm. Just as your thoughts and mind attract general things in your life, your desires are a great spiritual tool to attract spiritual things. Your desires are so powerful in attracting things that even God grants you what He sees that you desire.

Ps 37:4

Delight yourself also in the LORD, and He will give you the desires of your heart.

Ps 20:4

May He grant you according to your heart's *desire* and fulfil all your purpose.

If you aim for the prophetic anointing in your life, and your desire is pure and truthful, God will fulfil your purpose and give you your desire. I have realised that almost everything of the Spirit that we long for takes on an added and extreme importance. Whoever really wants to receive the things of the Spirit should long for them; desire precedes attainment.

This significance of desire explains why the apostle Paul encourages us to desire the best gifts of the Holy Spirit. He stresses that we must *earnestly desire the best gifts*. In the spiritual realm, it is the best gifts that we may attain and nothing of lesser significance.

> **1 COR 12:31**
>
> But earnestly desire the best gifts and yet I show you a more excellent way.

The above verse confirms again that what you desire is a vital tool to attract spiritual things. If you desire to operate with the grace of a kingdom financier, God will make you prosperous and give you opportunities to prove yourself in that field. If you want to function in a certain sphere of the Holy Spirit, the Bible encourages you to start desiring that gift for yourself.

Those who desire lesser things more than the greater things of God may come to harm. In Acts 5, for instance, Ananias holds back the proceeds from a land sale for himself, while donating only a portion to the church. By clinging to his own profits and disguising his motives, he lies to the Holy Spirit, which brings about his own death. Instead, if he had desired the greater things of God, he would have acted in harmony with the Holy Spirit for his own benefit and the benefit of God's people.

> **JOHN 7:37**
>
> On the last day, that great day of the feast, Jesus stood and cried out, saying, "If anyone thirsts, let him come to Me and drink".

Jesus Christ here is making an open call to receive water from Him; the only requirement is that whoever responds to the call has to be *thirsty.* There has to be a depth and intensity of thirst, and longing in the heart, for the thirst to be quenched and the longing met.

I urge you today to long and thirst for the prophetic anointing on your life, and to desire exactly that with purity and truth. If you want this anointing to operate within your life and upon you, your desire is the key.

Avail yourself

To "avail yourself" means to prepare yourself, mentally and physically, to be a pliable and willing tool in the hand of the Lord. Remember: every anointing is for service. Make yourself available to flow with the prophetic anointing, with which God has gifted you. Even if you believe and desire a good thing to manifest, you will unfortunately be deprived of it if you do not devote sufficient time to, or if you simply do not have the guts to handle, this holy and wonderful anointing.

For example, I love not merely traveling in a plane but actually flying one. Whenever I can, I spend time in the cockpit. I believe in flying and desire to fly. However, I have neither the time nor the will and dedication to avail myself of the necessary training to become a proficient pilot. If you desire to operate in the anointing of the Lord, allow Him to take control and to lead your life as He pleases. The only thing required of you is that you lay down your life on the altar as a living sacrifice.

Rom 12:1

I beseech you therefore, brethren, by the mercies of God, that you present your bodies a living sacrifice, holy, acceptable to God, *which is* your reasonable service.

The Rise of the Prophetic Voice

Many people want God to fit into their schedules instead of making themselves available to fit into God's schedule. Every great man and woman of God who has been used mightily by Him, surrendered everything, with trust and self-abandon, in order to make him or herself completely available to Him. The twelve apostles of Jesus Christ left everything that was theirs to make themselves available; no wonder they carried the first anointing for the gospel in the kingdom. By a groundbreaking event, they became the first apostles of the church of our Lord Jesus Christ.

> ## MATT 19:27
>
> Then Peter answered and said to Him, "See, we have left everything and followed You. Therefore what shall we have?"

Your availability will qualify you for the anointing. Remember that God knows that to give you what you are not available for would be a complete waste. Make yourself worthy of God's efforts and gifts.

Pay the price

It is important to state that the anointing requires huge sacrifice: *the anointing you have not paid the price for will never manifest in your life.* This sacrifice is especially challenging for most people. Many get discouraged from pursuing the anointing of God.

We live in a generation that wants everything given with no price paid. This generation specialises in shortcuts, and shortcuts short circuit all channels for anointing. You have to pay the *price* for the *prize.* As the saying goes, *a generation made of part-time Christians demands the service of a full-time God.* Today, even when we show no commitment to God and to the kingdom, we expect to enjoy their fullness, of which we read in the Scriptures. Remember: *only if we do what the Scriptures say we should do will we have what the Scriptures say we will have.*

I often meet people who ask to receive the same anointing that I have, and I keep telling them that it is easy to operate with an anointing upon your life, provided that you are ready to pay the required price and carry the necessary burden. The anointing requires commitment, consistency and hard work. You will learn to sanctify yourself and to travail in fasting and prayer. You must build yourself up by the Word and keep yourself diligent to it. You may expect to pay the price of obedience by doing what the Spirit asks of you, no matter how seemingly irrational or impractical.

Those who carry the anointing of God upon their lives do not live as most everyone else lives; instead, they live in full consecration and discipline.

Be in a prophetic environment

Saul's prophetic anointing manifested when he met a group of prophets. Their presence served as a prophetic environment for his anointing. Through this anointing, he prophesied.

It is of utmost importance that I emphasise, again, that many times God, in His supremacy, steps in to anoint any vessel He wants, to serve the prophetic at any given time and for whichever the specific assignment. In Numbers 22, God tries to communicate with His servant Balaam; He prophetically anoints His animal: "a donkey whose eyes mysteriously opened to see what he himself could not see and even spoke like a man would speak". The story in full goes like this:

NUM 22:21-32

So Balaam rose in the morning, saddled his donkey, and went with the princes of Moab. Then God's anger was aroused because he went, and the Angel of the Lord took His stand in the way as an adversary against him. And he was riding on his donkey, and his two servants

---

were with him. Now the donkey saw the Angel of the Lord standing in the way with His drawn sword in His hand, and the donkey turned aside out of the way and went into the field. So Balaam struck the donkey to turn her back onto the road. Then the Angel of the Lord stood in a narrow path between the vineyards, with a wall on this side and a wall on that side. And when the donkey saw the Angel of the Lord, she pushed herself against the wall and crushed Balaam's foot against the wall; so he struck her again. Then the Angel of the Lord went further, and stood in a narrow place where there was no way to turn either to the right hand or to the left. And when the donkey saw the Angel of the Lord, she lay down under Balaam; so Balaam's anger was aroused, and he struck the donkey with his staff. Then the Lord opened the mouth of the donkey, and she said to Balaam, "What have I done to you, that you have struck me these three times?" And Balaam said to the donkey, "Because you have abused me. I wish there were a sword in my hand, for now I would kill you!" So the donkey said to Balaam, "Am I not your donkey on which you have ridden, ever since I became yours, to this day? Was I ever disposed to do this to you?" And he said, "No". Then the Lord opened Balaam's eyes, and he saw the Angel of the Lord standing in the way with His drawn sword in His hand; and he bowed his head and fell flat on his face. And the Angel of the Lord said to him, "Why have you struck your donkey these three times? Behold, I have come out to stand against you, because your way is perverse before Me."

What is the meaning of this? Do donkeys naturally see in the spirit or have a hidden ability to speak the languages of men? Do we consider donkeys to be prophetic animals? Before you rush off to buy yourself a donkey on a farm near you, please allow me to tell you that no donkey has a natural ability to see into the spiritual realm or to speak the intelligible languages of men. Donkeys are not prophets; they are beautiful animals just like all the other animals created by God.

The story in Numbers 22 recounts a special event where God miraculously anoints a donkey in order to minister to His servant

(Balaam) who is going the wrong way. This story illustrates the prophetic anointing. The prophetic anointing operates by coming upon someone for the sake of a specific assignment. The anointing affords the recipient the same tools and abilities as those of normal prophets.

The Gift of Prophecy

Besides the prophetic anointing, which may operate for any child of God, the New Testament describes an *office* of the prophet and a *gift* of prophecy. These two prophetic capacities are significant.

Those who occupy the office of the prophet do so by calling, while those who have the gift of prophecy are equipped with a permanent prophetic tool or ability. Both groups are children of God or servants of God. Just as the possession of a machine gun (say, at home) does not automatically make someone a soldier enrolled in the national army, so the possession of a prophetic gift does not automatically make someone a prophet of God, enrolled in God's special forces.

You can be a worshipper with a prophetic gift, or an elder or deacon in a church with a prophetic gift. An usher or intercessor, an evangelist or a pastor, may all have prophetic gifts. The Holy Spirit gives the prophetic gift to all different kinds of people in different walks of life.

---

1 COR 12:11

But one and the same Spirit works all these things, distributing to each one individually as He wills.

However, not everyone with a prophetic gift or prophetic anointing can occupy the office of the prophet. Ephesians 4 speaks of the office of the prophet:

> **EPH 4:11**
>
> And He Himself gave some to be apostles, some prophets, some evangelists, and some pastors and teachers.

1 Corinthians 14 speaks of the gift of prophecy:

> **1 COR 14:31**
>
> For you can all prophesy one by one, that all may learn and all may be encouraged.

These verses imply that the doors for accessing the gift of prophecy are open to everyone, as the Spirit Himself wills. Desire is not sufficient for the gift of prophecy, although your earnest desire will position you for that gift, provided that the Holy Spirit decides to give it to you. The Holy Spirit alone has the last word. Paul's First Letter to the Corinthians, chapter 14, offers a great deal of insight into the gift of prophecy.

> **1 COR 14:1**
>
> Pursue love and desire spiritual *gifts*, but especially that you may prophesy.

> **1 COR 14:5**
>
> I wish you all spoke with tongues but even more that you prophesied, for he who prophesies *is* greater than he who speaks with tongues, unless indeed he interprets, that the church may receive edification.

> ## 1 Cor 14:24-25
>
> But if all prophesy and an unbeliever or an uninformed person comes in, he is convinced by all, he is convicted by all. And thus the secrets of his heart are revealed; and so falling down on *his* face, he will worship God and report that God is truly among you.

> ## 1 Cor 14:39
>
> Therefore brethren, desire earnestly to prophesy, and do not forbid to speak with tongues.

A careful reading of the Scriptures gives rise to the realisation that the gift of prophecy is somehow limited in its operation, as compared to the office of the prophet.

In 1 Corinthians 14 prophecy is defined as a means for edification, exhortation and comfort. The Amplified Bible for 1 Cor 14: 3 says:

> The one who prophesies speaks to people for edification [to promote their spiritual growth] and [speaks words of] encouragement [to uphold and advise them concerning the matters of God] and [speaks words of] consolation [to compassionately comfort them].

The capacity to predict the future is not, here, essential to the gift of prophecy. However, prediction is one main function of the prophetic office. The gift of prophecy is directed mainly to building up the local church but, in some select instances, the gift of prophecy expresses itself in a deeper and more symbolic way, through the revelation of secrets and by accurate predictions of certain future events.

> ## ACTS 15:32
>
> Now Judas and Silas, themselves being prophets also, exhorted and strengthened the brethren with many words.

Here, Judas and Silas are mentioned as *also being prophets*; the ancient term for prophets, which is used here, means that they also operate in the prophetic. The verse could be expressed this way: *Now Judas and Silas, themselves also being prophetic, exhorted and strengthened the brethren with many words.*

We know clearly in Scripture that both Judas and Silas were involved in the apostolic ministry, but in the text above it is revealed that they also carried the prophetic gift. They were able to exhort and to strengthen the brethren with many words.

The gift of prophecy operates according to the anointing of the Spirit of God. The prophet is heavily anointed so as to speak forth to the Body of Christ, not in premeditated or prepared words, but rather by words that the Spirit Himself supplies, spontaneously to uplift and to encourage, to incite others to faithful obedience and service, and to bring comfort and consolation. The gift of prophecy may accord the prophet access to a great revelation or vision about which he can speak with accuracy. In its main function, however, the prophetic gift builds up and edifies the local church.

It is also important to mention that, when one operates with the gift of prophecy, one does not have complete control over its operation. The prophetic office provides greater control. I can prophesy literally as I can speak. But those with prophetic gifts might not always flow with such ease and consistency. The emphasis in the ministry of the prophets, in the Old and New Testaments, is not limited to prediction. The prophet is dedicated to setting forth clearly what God has said, in whatever form that takes.

---

1 COR 2:9

But as it is written: "Eye has not seen, nor ear heard, nor have entered into the heart of man the things which God has prepared for those who love Him".

The Greek word, which is translated as *prophesying* (verb) or *prophecy* (noun), means to *speak forth* or to *speak on behalf of*. In prophecy, one declares the revealed Word of God. The Greek word for prophecy (noun) *propheteia* entails the ability to receive a divinely-inspired message and to deliver it to others.

The prophetic gift is a concrete tool, a special spiritual skill, a supernatural ability in the Spirit, to receive messages from God for His people and the world. With the gift of prophecy, you are able to operate on a level just below the fully ordained prophet of God. Any believer can operate with the gift of prophecy provided that he or she is chosen and endowed by the Holy Spirit. A full-time minister called in a different five-fold ministry can also have the gift of prophecy for his own ministry.

There are evangelists, pastors, teachers and apostles in the Body of Christ today, who carry and manifest the gift of prophecy. I personally know of pastors and teachers with a strong gift of prophecy. This gift has come in handy in assisting their ministries, in many ways, to be effective and impactful. The combination of the gift of prophecy with any other ministry, operating in the Body of Christ, is so dynamic that it may mightily reveal the glory of God amongst men.

A gospel music artist whom I know, attracts many to his concerts and "praise and worship" events, not just because of the songs and vibes, but also thanks to the prophetic ministration that goes with his ministry. He is not a prophet; his primary call is to lead the Body of Christ in praise and worship. He is so prophetic, however, that sometimes he interrupts his songs in a concert and gets off the stage to minister prophetically to people in the audience. His songs are also full of spontaneous prophetic messages, which are direct and accurate, thus making his ministry effective in touching and changing lives.

The gift of prophecy is listed in 1 Corinthians 12 as one of the gifts of the Holy Spirit:

1 COR 12:4-11

There are diversities of gifts, but the same Spirit. There are differences of ministries, but the same Lord. And there are diversities of activities, but it is the same God who works all in all. But the manifestation of the Spirit is given to each one for the profit *of all:* **for to one is given the word of wisdom through the Spirit, to another the word of knowledge through the same Spirit, to another faith by the same**

Spirit, to another gifts of healings by] the same Spirit, to another the working of miracles, to another prophecy, to another discerning of spirits, to another *different* **kinds of tongues, to another the interpretation of tongues.** But one and the same Spirit works all these things, distributing to each one individually as He wills.

The gift of prophecy is one of the nine gifts of the Holy Spirit listed in 1 Corinthians 12. In the same letter of Corinthians, Paul speaks about the gift of prophecy, comparing it to the gift of tongues.

> ## 1 COR 14:1-5
>
> Pursue love, and desire spiritual *gifts*, but especially that you may prophesy. For he who speaks in a tongue does not speak to men but to God, for no one understands *him*; however, in the spirit he speaks mysteries. But he who prophesies speaks edification and exhortation and comfort to men. He who speaks in a tongue edifies himself, but he who prophesies edifies the church. I wish you all spoke with tongues, but even more that you prophesied; for he who prophesies *is* greater than he who speaks with tongues, unless indeed he interprets, that the church may receive edification.

Let us boldly acknowledge that the Bible openly speaks of the gift of prophecy as one of the gifts of the Holy Spirit given to the church today. There should be no debate as to whether the gift of prophecy is biblical. The sixth gift of the Holy Spirit listed in 1 Corinthians 12 is the gift of prophecy. A *gift* is *something given willingly to someone without payment.* The gift of prophecy is a tool given freely to an individual by the Holy Spirit of God. On many different occasions, we have probably received gifts from family, friends and loved ones, so we understand perfectly well the concept of a gift. Gifts are not limited to material things; rather, they include special abilities, talents or skills that God allots to each one of us, individually.

Great soccer players, for instance, are clearly born with a talent, a gift for soccer. Their general facility and passion for this ball game exceed the range and intensity of passion for the sport of the average person. Considerable investment and training are required to make one's talent or gift shine. But, training by itself does not make someone a *King Pele* or a *Diego Maradona.* Nevertheless, it should not be discounted that training remains the key for developing the best skills. Many were born with greater potential than King Pele, most likely, but they remain unknown and unsuccessful today, for lack of effort in developing their talents through training. Personal qualities are also crucial to success, such as courage, sacrifice, determination, commitment, persistence and discipline. Gifts come before training; without a gift, training may not take someone anywhere.

Talent is defined as a natural ability. For example, some people are good at singing; even at a young age, they can sing beautifully. Their talent is a natural gift and an aptitude from within. *Leo Buscaglia* said, "Your talent is God's gift to you. What you do with it is your gift back to God."

Now the gift of prophecy is a supernatural ability, given freely to a believer by the Holy Spirit to enable him or her to see and hear in the spiritual realm. Those who have received this gift are able to operate prophetically in the church, by seeing and hearing in the supernatural realm and by announcing and predicting future events. Through these gifts, they serve as God's spokespersons.

Unlike the prophetic anointing, the prophetic gift is permanent. Once you have it, you will always have it. Someone told me once that he had lost his gift. I explained to him that he did not lose the gift but rather its functionality. This loss may occur due to distraction, sinful behaviour or a lack of focus and investment in your gift. It may seem to you that the gift has died. But the truth is that, once you start doing things right again, the same gift will be revived and will resurface in your life.

Rom 11:29

For the gifts and the calling of God *are* irrevocable.

This scripture is true for salvation and for any other God-given gift. All His gifts to us are irrevocable. We should *resurrect* our gifts or they will remain dormant and be rendered completely useless to us and to everyone else.

How Do We Acquire the Gift of Prophecy?

The gift of prophecy reveals the presence of God to His people in an outstanding way. Where the gift of prophecy is operational, the presence of God becomes so tangible that reverence for Him, among people, soars – and their dedication becomes natural.

The apostle Paul held that the gift of prophecy is higher than that of tongues, and I presume also higher than certain other gifts recorded in the Scriptures. In 1 Corinthians 14, he mentions his wish that everyone might prophesy, implying that the prophetic gift is not an exclusive or elite privilege in the Body of Christ, belonging to those who are born different or who are of a certain breed and breeding.

> ## 1 COR 14:5
>
> I wish you all spoke with tongues, but even more that you prophesied;] for he who prophesies is greater than he who speaks with tongues, unless indeed he interprets, that the church may receive edification.

But the question remains: How do we acquire this gift? The answer is found in 1 Corinthians 12. The first thing I must underline is that the gifts of the Spirit are given to us *by the Holy Spirit.*

> ## 1 COR 12:11
>
> But one and the same Spirit works all these things, distribut- ing to each one individually as He wills.

So, whoever wants the gift of prophecy should plead with the Holy Spirit, who distributes spiritual gifts amongst believers according to His own will. Spiritual gifts can be transferred from one person to another through impartation. One who carries a fatherly anointing can impart his gift to a person desiring it. The Holy Spirit will lead him in this kind of service for the sake of ministry. The Scriptures describe such transfers:

> ### ROM 1:11
>
> For I long to see you, that I may impart to you some spiritual gift, so that you may be established.

In the above scripture, Paul is expressing a desire to see the believers in Rome *so that he may impart to them some spiritual gift.* To impart means to bestow, to give, to deposit, to communicate. Only someone who carries spiritual authority over you, like your father in the Lord, can do this impartation (I believe). Paul was the apostle used by God to establish the believers in Rome; their spiritual umbilical cords were linked to him. Paul imparted spiritual gifts to believers not only in Rome but across his ministry. In 2 Tim 1:6-7, the figure of Paul does the same to Timothy, his spiritual son, and he reminds Timothy to keep on working with the gift imparted.

> ### 2 TIM 1:6-7
>
> Therefore I remind you to stir up the gift of God which is in you through the laying on of my hands.

Many times, the Spirit of God has permitted me to impart the gifts of the Holy Spirit, which are within me, to my spiritual sons and daughters from around the world. By the grace of God, I am blessed to operate with all nine gifts of the Holy Spirit listed in 1 Corinthians 12. That I am being used by the Holy Spirit to impart different gifts to God's children is an amazing grace. I do not count myself as someone of superior value; it truly humbles me deeply to recognise that God will, here and there, use me – of all people – to fulfil a task in the kingdom and to be a blessing to His people. I am truly grateful.

A pastor, suffering great setbacks, was on the verge of closing his ministry when he was led to submit to God under me. God had told him, he said, that I carry His blessing and that he should connect with me for his breakthrough. He started attending most of my special programmes in ministry, and some Sundays he would leave his church to come to my church service. He said that he was told that I would, at least, pray for him in the auditorium during the time of ministration to the people. After a while, he began to doubt that this prayer would happen, given the size of the crowd in church.

One day, though, while I was praying for him and the people in the church, I was led to minister. God asked me to impart to him the gift of prophecy and healing. From that day on, nothing remains the same in his life: his ministry has taken off to great heights. It happened almost immediately. God is using him to touch and change lives out there by His grace. In the space of three months, his church growth has been unbelievable. He has grown from 40 to 600 people and today there are close to 2000 people in his ministry. Apart from his congregation, God is using him in different soul-wining events around the country, and testimonies are mind-blowing to say the least.

The fatherly anointing is a special privilege. (As the Lord permits, I will share more about this anointing in another book.) Those who carry such anointing are able to transfer whatever they carry as spiritual gifts to those under their spiritual jurisdiction. To a degree, everyfather carries that anointing at a basic level. There are different levels of fatherly anointing. Fatherly anointing may cover only one or two people, who are very close to you, or it may cover an entire generation. Just as a house may have a father, so a generation may have fathers. May God raise fathers in our generation. The concept of father designates "source". A real father is a source of wisdom, blessings, spiritual strength, spiritual gifts and much more.

Having said this, the main way to go about receiving the gift of the prophecy is through *eagerly desiring* it.

---

1 COR 12:31

But earnestly desire the best gifts. And yet I show you a more excellent way.

To *eagerly desire* means to desire deeply, enthusiastically and zealously; not to merely want the gift of prophecy but to burn inside for it. Desire is indispensable for receiving the prophetic anointing. Desire applies similarly as a prerequisite for obtaining the gift of prophecy.

The Prophetic Call or the Prophetic Ministry

It is important to assert that there is a difference between the ministry of the prophet and the gift of prophecy. Having a gift of prophecy does not make you automatically a prophet. *The prophetic ministry is a call*; it is like all the other ministries of our Lord Jesus Christ as mentioned in the five-fold ministry.

---

1 COR 1: 26-27

For you see your calling, brethren, that not many wise according to the flesh, not many mighty, not many noble, *are called.* But God has chosen the foolish things of the world to put to shame the wise, and God has chosen the weak things of the world to put to shame the things which are mighty.

> ## 1 COR 7:20
> Let each one remain in the same calling in which he was called.

The Bible differentiates between a call and a gift. A call speaks of your vocation, your life assignment, your mission, and your reason for being, but a gift is a special ability given to you to excel at a specific task.

Every one of us has a God-given calling in life. God created us all for a purpose, and though our life purpose or callings may differ from person to person, they are all important and strategic in fulfilling the perfect will of God on earth. Some are called to a priesthood or ministry; they become apostles, prophets, teachers, pastors and evangelists. Others are called to different things in the Body of Christ and in life in general. Every calling comes from God and advances His agenda on earth through the kingdom.

Mother Teresa observed that many people mistake their career for their calling.* We are so acquainted with our careers in life that at times we confuse our careers with our calling.

Paul was called to be an apostle by the will of God, but he was a tent maker in his career (Acts 18:3). Some people have managed to align their careers completely to match their callings, while others have kept them completely separate. For example, someone who is called to be an author and has made a career in publishing books may have managed to combine their calling with a career in publishing.

For the first ten years of our ministry, I was the senior pastor of the church but I had a full-time job in a corporate field. I was the group's managing director of a company in Johannesburg with listed

---

* Exact source unknown.

interests in the London Stock Exchange; I was also the CEO of a petroleum company, undertaking exploration projects in on- and off-shore locations. I was combining ministry and my secular job. On the one hand, I was fulfilling my calling; on the other hand, I was pursuing a career. This duality continued until the Lord finally told me to focus only on the work of my calling. Combining your calling and career when they are different in nature is not a bad thing but might become a handicap at some point.

Your calling defines what you are supposed to do in this life. Therefore, it is of paramount importance. Unless you know the reason for your existence, what you have been designed by God to be and to do on earth, you are a lost cause with no direction. So I ask these questions: "Why did God create you?" "Why do you exist?" "Do you know the purpose of your life?" "What does God expect from your life that is different from what He expects from everyone else?"

If you are not able to answer these questions correctly, you may not know your real calling; neither do you know your purpose or your vocation. No matter what you do with your life, nothing meaningful will come from it without a secure sense of calling. You may otherwise live your life, trying to imitate people and to be someone that you are not. You will likely experience a lot of instability and try many things without success by gambling away your resources, in your search for what truly fits your purpose on earth.

Honoré de Balzac said, "An unfulfilled calling drains the colour from a man's entire existence".*

You will never have a sense of fulfilment without knowing and walking according to what God has designed you for. Fulfilment

---

* See: https://www. goodreads. com/quotes/74968-an-unfulfilled-vocation-drains-the-color-from-a-man-s-entire

comes from achieving what is set before you; you must run your own race, *not someone else's race*. I was designed by God not to be a medical doctor, an engineer, a politician or a pilot. I have been created to be an authorised mouthpiece of God, an oracle of the Lord and a prophet of nations in this generation. If, today, I decided to become a medical doctor simply because I like helping those who are sick, I would be doing myself a great disservice and robbing the world of the best of me, which they can only get if I do what I am called for in life.

You can only truly excel in what you are called for by God because every capacity you have in you is meant to help you fulfil what you are called for. Your mission is given based on what you are called for; your gifts, talents and skills are also given to you to assist you. The opportunities that you will come across in life allow you to develop your calling and the purposes that God has in mind for you.

Thomas Merton said, "For each one of us, there is only one thing necessary: to fulfil our destiny according to God's will; to be what He called us to be".*

Knowing your calling will position you to achieve what is set before you. There would be less competition in the Body of Christ if we each knew what we were called for and how we should fulfil our individual callings.

The call of God in your life cannot be upgraded or changed. You cannot be called into full-time ministry today and change to a different calling altogether tomorrow. Some are called into evangelism and, after a while, they get bored evangelising. They decide to join a more fashionable calling; they become apostles or teachers. You are called to be a missionary and to preach the gospel

---

* From Thomas Merton, *No Man is an Island*, see: https://www. goodreads. com/quotes/564411-for-each-one-of-us-there-is-only-one-thing

The Rise of the Prophetic Voice

but, while on the field of the Lord, you come across lucrative business opportunities; you upgrade your calling from being a missionary to being a businessman. When asked about your mission, you reply that through financing the gospel you are still doing your mission work. But God knows that is not true; you have simply deviated from the call of God in your life.

> **1 COR 7:20**
>
> Let each one remain in the same calling in which he was called.

You should stick to the calling of God in your life no matter what. Do not suppose that what you are called to be and to do in life is not good enough.

Thomas Merton said, "A man knows when he has found his vocation when he stops thinking about how to live and begins to live".*

It is true that sometimes the calling of God in our lives may unfold slowly and, in the process, assume different shapes and forms. For example, you may be called into the pastoral ministry, but for the first *ten years* of your Christian life you find yourself operating as a worship leader. During those years, you may have to build yourself a reputation as a worshipper; later, the Lord may reveal to you that you are to be in a full-time pastoral ministry. That new role does not change your initial calling; instead, you are growing in the will of God as far as your calling is concerned. I have seen people who started serving God as evangelists and later were established in the pastorate or apostolic ministry. This happens because sometimes God may take you through a process away from your calling – in order to prepare you for it.

---

* See: https://www. goodreads. com/quotes/114483-a-man-knows-when-he-has-found-his-vocation-when

The Calling

> ## 1 COR 1:26-27
>
> For you see your calling, brethren, that not many wise according to the flesh, not many mighty, not many noble, *are called*. But God has chosen the foolish things of the world to put to shame the wise, and God has chosen the weak things of the world to put to shame the things which are mighty.

> ## GAL 1:15
>
> But when it pleased God, who separated me from my mother's womb and called me through His grace.

> ## JER 1:5
>
> Before I formed you in the womb I knew you; before you were born, I sanctified you; I ordained you a prophet to the nations.

> ## EPH 4:1
>
> I, therefore, the prisoner of the Lord, beseech you to walk worthy of the calling with which you were called.

How do you know if you are called to operate with the prophetic anointing, or the prophetic gift, or whether you are called into a full prophetic ministry?

As mentioned earlier, not knowing what your God-given calling is will result in a great deal of confusion and lack of performance in the exercise of your life assignment. However, the question in many people's minds is how to know what you are truly called for or which gift of the Holy Spirit you have.

There are many ways presented to us as a means to identify what you are called for and what you carry in you; here, I want to present you with *three* effective ways to discover what you are called for. Let me start by telling you that there may be non-conclusive signs that you are called for something or that you have a specific gift from God.

Non-conclusive Signs of Your Call or Gift

The non-conclusive signs are your abilities or capacities and your desires.

Abilities and capacities

Having natural abilities and capacities to do something easily is not a definite sign that you are called for it. Everyone has different natural abilities that can be used to successfully do a number of things.

You are not called to driving simply because you can drive your car easily and safely from one point to another. God has given each one of us many abilities and capacities in various fields of life but those abilities or capacities are not always the vital signs of our callings.

For example, you can cook a meal but your calling might not be to become a professional cook. You swim well, but your calling may not be in swimming but in football. Being eloquent is not a sign that you are called into full-time ministry as a preacher or a teacher. Often, those who are called by God are fearful. Even knowing God has called them to service, they feel small, incapable of fulfilling the task. They lack strength or ability and have no crutch on which to lean.

Moses objected to God, explaining that he had a *stammer*, and so he was unable to accept the call to deliver Israel. *Gideon* said to God that he was unable to carry out the task of his calling because he was the smallest in his family, which meant the smallest in the tribe. *Jeremiah* said to God that he was too young for the call and therefore unable to execute it.

Your natural ability is not necessarily the indication of your calling. To fulfil your God-given calling, you will need more than your natural ability, your talent and your skills; you will need supernatural empowerment.

God does not call the qualified but qualifies the called.

Desires

A *desire* is a strong feeling of want, whether to have something or to wish for an event to happen. Can your desire be an indication that you are called to a specific ministry or that you have a specific call of God in your life or a gift? God never undermines your desires, as the Bible promises in Psalm 37:

Ps 37:4

Delight yourself also in the Lord, And He shall give you the desires of your heart.

The desires of those who delight in the Lord are often created by God as an attraction for what He has reserved for them. It is common knowledge that, in the prophetic, the Holy Spirit may use our desires to draw us to something according to His plan. When it comes to the gift of the Holy Spirit, we are permitted to desire the best gift. In prayer, the Holy Spirit may be given to us, for the Holy Spirit itself is the best gift.

> **1 Cor 12:31**
>
> But earnestly desire the best gifts. And yet I show you a more excellent way.

We should *desire* the best gifts. But does this mean that our desire is an indication of our calling or gifting in God? No, absolutely not. Our desires are not enough to stand as an absolute sign of our calling or our gift in God.

The mere fact that you want to be a singer does not automatically imply that you were born to sing. Your desire to become a singer, in this case, may derive from a strong liking and appreciation of music. Time after time, I meet people who tell me how they desire to go into full-time ministry; most of them mean well. They want to be in full-time ministry even at the cost of their careers and current occupations. They do not mind losing their source of income for this cause and they are ready to jump into full-time ministry blindfolded. Though this sounds like a fine and worthy pursuit, it is often a grave mistake to embark on such a permanent change, based simply on the fact of your desire.

To understand your call in God, you will need to rely on more than the direction given you by your desires. There are two important ways to know and discover your call and gift in God: inner conviction and revelation by the Holy Ghost

Inner voice

There is always a witness within you that speaks to you about what God has destined for your life; if you pay attention to that small, convincing voice, you will find in yourself what you were born for. Your inner *you* knows better than your intellect may know.

What is it that led Moses to intervene when he came across an Egyptian who was hurting an Israelite? What led him to kill the Egyptian in the process? The following day, the Bible says that he came across two Israelites fighting one another, and he intervened again, but this time he was trying to stop the fight. Was it just coincidence that pushed him to intervene again when he saw those two Israelites fighting one another? No. Though Moses could not himself understand what was happening, he was in fact being led by his inner being to do what he was born for. He was preparing to become the deliverer of Israel.

It is important for us all to understand that the day when we gave our lives to Jesus, He regenerated and restored us. Our spiritual being is now reunited with our God and is therefore our true being. I am not referring to the Spirit of God or the Holy Ghost but rather to our own human spirit. *A man is a spirit that has a soul and lives in a body.*

Our spirit is deep within us, which the Scriptures call our inner being. The spirit often speaks to us from within and gives us clarity and direction on vital matters. Many of us neglect the fact that our spirit communicates to our renewed mind things that our intellect will never be able to comprehend; as a result we do not pay attention.

You can know the purpose of your existence by just listening to your inner voice. The voice of our inner man might sometimes be contrary to our natural aspirations; it may sometimes sound crazy and irrational, but it is often the voice of reason within our being. So listen to it.

Revelation by the Holy Ghost

Revelation is the easiest way to know what you are called for. In the Word of God, most of those called by God receive their calling by revelation or a spiritual encounter with God. Through revelation,

The Rise of the Prophetic Voice

mysteries about the purpose of your existence and details of your calling may be revealed. Such a revelation may come to you directly or through someone else, but either way it is important to have two or three confirmations before you consider the revelation established.

For example, should you receive a personal revelation that you are called to serve God in such and such ministry, it is important to wait for confirmation from two or three trustworthy people before you venture into what you believe has been revealed. The same applies if you have received a prophetic word or a revelation informing you of your calling; it is important to wait for one or two confirmations before jumping into the new thing. This is to ensure that you do not make a mistake. The Bible says:

> **DEUT 17:6**
>
> Whoever is deserving of death shall be put to death on the testimony of two or three witnesses; he shall not be put to death on the testimony of one witness.

> **DEUT 19:15**
>
> One witness shall not rise against a man concerning any iniquity or any sin that he commits; by the mouth of two or three witnesses the matter shall be established.

The above scriptures refer to a law in Israel that required more than one witness before a matter was verified and concluded. The report or testimony of one person was deemed insufficient for a final verdict; the law stated that a report of two or three witnesses would be required before the matter was concluded. It was as a precaution and a matter of prudence that this law was established.

The principle of this law is extremely important for matters of the kingdom. Today, biblical scholars use it as a way to know what in the Scripture is doctrinal truth for us to follow and what is not. So, whenever you receive a revelation pertaining to your calling, wait for the confirmation of God.

You may feel that to wait for confirmation will be a waste of time, but understand that it is best to wait rather than to commit for a possible lifetime to error. Besides, if God is truly speaking to you, He won't mind confirming His Word. Revelation is the most direct and easiest way to know your call or gift in God. Many great men and women of God in the Bible have discovered their calling and assignment through a direct revelation.

Moses

Ex 3:1-7

Now Moses was tending the flock of Jethro his father-in-law, the priest of Midian. And he led the flock to the back of the desert, and cameto Horeb, the mountain of God. And the Angel of the Lord appeared to him in a flame of fire from the midst of a bush. So he looked, and behold, the bush was burning with fire, but the bush was not consumed. Then Moses said, "I will now turn aside and see this great sight, why the bush does not burn". So when the Lord saw that he turned aside to look, God called to him from the midst of the bush and said, "Moses, Moses!"And he said, "Here I am". Then He said, "Do not draw near this place. Take your sandals off your feet, for the place where you stand is holy ground." Moreover He said, "I am the God of your father – the God of Abraham, the God of Isaac, and the God of Jacob". And Moses hid his face, for he was afraid to look upon God. And the Lord said: "I have surely seen the oppression of My people who are in Egypt, and have heard their cry because of their taskmasters, for I know their sorrows".

In this famous and pivotal moment, a theophany occurs, a manifestation of God through a sensory medium on earth. There is a theophany on Mt Sinai, too. Earlier, Moses witnesses a theophany through a burning bush.

Moses had been taking care of the flocks belonging to his father-in-law when he saw a bush, which was burning but not consumed. He drew near to this unusual phenomenon. There he had an encounter with God. He heard a voice commanding him to remove his sandals for he was standing on holy ground. God spoke to him about His people of Israel, about their sufferings and His plan for their liberation.

From there Moses was no longer a shepherd working for his father-in-law; he discovered his calling and mission. He took his family and went back to Egypt to deliver the children of Israel.

Saul

1 Sam 9:1-27; 1 Sam 10:1

Saul, son of Kish, went looking for the lost donkeys of his father. He searched everywhere and could not find them. On the advice of his servant, he decided to go to consult Samuel the prophet in quest of finding his father's lost donkeys. When he met the prophet, his personal calling was revealed to him and the prophet anointed him to be king over Israel.

He came to know his calling by revelation and so he became the first king of Israel.

David

1 Sam 16:1-13

David, son of Jesse, was following behind the flocks of his father when it was revealed to the prophet Samuel that he had been chosen by God to become the next king of Israel.

David had no clue that he had been called to be king of Israel, but that was revealed to him, and in the appointed time he became king over Israel and reigned for forty years.

Acts 9:6

So he, trembling and astonished, said, "Lord, what do You want me to do?" Then the Lord *said* to him, "Arise and go into the city, and you will be told what you must do".

Paul

Paul's conversion occurred through a spectacular happening on his way to persecute the church. He had an encounter with our Lord Jesus that led him to repentance and directed his steps to his ministry. God used Ananias to reveal to him his calling and to prepare him for it.

My Experience

I gave my life to Jesus Christ at a very tender age, and I have since fully dedicated myself to walking with God. I always had an inner witness within me that attested to the fact that I would serve God. Different men and women of God prophesied that God would use me in a very special way. Some members of my family received messages concerning my calling from different servants of God, but I never understood the complete meaning of them. Two years after I gave my life to God, *the Spirit of God revealed to me clearly what my calling was.* Of course, I was terrified as I felt it was a *mission impossible.* It took me two years before I surrendered to God and said *yes* to His call in my life.

So, in conclusion, there are two important ways to discover the call of God in your life: through your inner voice (the voice of your inner being or the Spirit) and through a revelation. Some people have discovered their callings through one of the two, but others have experienced both modes of confirmation, regarding their God-given calling.

Now the question remains: *How to know whether you have just a prophetic anointing, a prophetic gift, or whether you are in reality a prophet.*

Every child of God who is open to the Holy Spirit is a worthy candidate for the *prophetic anointing* in his or her life and can be prophetic. To be prophetic simply means that your mind and spirit are connected to the prophetic moves of God; you believe, accept, and open yourself to these prophetic moves. You are aligned with the Spirit with the attitude of a prophet.

One of the easiest ways to know the nature of what you have in you is to check its fruits. Jesus said, "You shall know them by their fruits," meaning that the fruits reveal the very nature of the tree that produced them (Luke 6:43-45).

Know If You Have a Prophetic Anointing

Though the prophetic anointing can enable you to prophesy on some occasions, it primarily works for you by making you a prophet over your own destiny. When it manifests in you, you will notice that there is a sort of *invisible guider* in your life, which leads you to the right thing at the right time and effortlessly wards off serious issues. You will not be able to pinpoint what it is, but you will recognise this guiding force.

The word of the Psalmist becomes more real when you operate with a prophetic anointing:

> **Ps 37:23**
>
> The steps of a *good* **man are ordered by the Lord,** And He delights in his way.

Have you ever felt a strong and urgent urge to pray for someone or something, or to check on someone or something and it turns out that it was crucial and timely? If yes, this might be an indication of the prophetic anointing on you.

Have you ever, out of the blue, had a bad feeling about something or someone and it turns out that you were right? Well, you may be operating with a prophetic anointing. It may seem like a simple result of your gut feel, your intuition, or just coincidence, but it is not; it is the prophetic manifesting in you.

Do you often see things in your dreams and they somehow happen? They are dreams that happen under the prophetic anointing; such dreams are meaningful messages from God to guide, warn and correct us. If you often dream of things that happen, you may be operating with a prophetic anointing. There are lives that have been saved by prophetic dreams. And prophetic dreams are among the manifestations of the prophetic anointing.

A dream is a language or a means of communication from your spirit to your soul. Just as the body has a language – "body language" – so the Spirit in you has a language through which it communicates to your soul. The Spirit conveys vital information from the spiritual realm. Your soul is the part of you that represents your personality on earth. It is made up of three essential parts: your *mind* (your thinking, rationality, intelligence), your *will* (your wants, your desires), and your *emotions* (your feelings). When it comes to dreams, your Spirit receives spiritual information and conveys it to your soul (*mind, will* and *emotions*) through pictures. Some of them are clear while others come in codes and enigmas and therefore require interpretation.

Many in the Bible received vital information from God through dreams. This is how prophetic dreams come about: your human soul through a prophetic anointing is enabled to receive information from God. The message is passed on to you in the form of images and pictures that we call dreams. The Bible reports of many people – both in the Old and New Testaments – who prophetically received messages from God in dreams; they were not necessarily prophets themselves, but through the work of the prophetic anointing, bestowed on them, they were guided.

Here are some verses about people who received prophetic messages through dreams:

GEN 15:1

After these things the word of the LORD came to Abram in a vision, saying, "Do not be afraid, Abram. *I am* your shield, your exceedingly great reward".

GEN 28:12

Then he dreamed, and behold, a ladder was set up on the earth, and its top reached to heaven; and there the angels of God were ascending and descending on it.

GEN 37:5

Now Joseph had a dream and he told *it* to his brothers; and they hated him all the more.

GEN 46:2

God spoke to Israel in the visions of the night, and said, "Jacob, Jacob!" And he said, "Here I am".

JUD 7:13-15

And when Gideon had come, there was a man telling a dream to his companion. He said, "I have had a dream: To my surprise, a loaf of barley bread tumbled into the camp of Midian; it came to a tent and struck it so that it fell and overturned, and the tent collapsed." Then his companion answered and said, "This is nothing else but the sword of Gideon the son of Joash, a man of Israel! Into his hand God has delivered Midian and the whole camp." And so it was, when Gideon heard the telling of the dream and its interpretation, that he worshipped. He returned to the camp of Israel, and said, "Arise, for the Lord has delivered the camp of Midian into your hand".

DAN 4:5

I saw a dream which made me afraid, and the thoughts on my bed and the visions of my head troubled me.

> ## DAN 7:1
>
> In the first year of Belshazzar king of Babylon, Daniel had a dream and visions of his head *while* **on his bed. Then he wrote down the dream, telling the main facts.**

> ## MATT 2:12
>
> Then, being divinely warned in a dream that they should not return to Herod, they departed for their own country another way.

> ## ACTS 22:17-18
>
> Now it happened, when I returned to Jerusalem and was praying in the temple, that I was in a trance. And I saw him saying to me, make haste, and get out of Jerusalem quickly, for they will not receive your testimony concerning Me.

Prophetic dreams are frequent in the lives of those who operate with the prophetic anointing. In the Old Testament, even unlikely figures are reported to have received prophetic dreams: Pharaoh, King of Egypt (Gen 41:1) and Nebuchadnezzar, the great King of Babylon (Dan 2:28).

Know If You Have a Gift of Prophecy

The gift of prophecy has to do with the ability to speak forth the revealed Word of God, which sends a message to someone or for some purpose. The *gift of prophecy* gives you the ability to know things through means that are not explicable from a natural perspective. Things will be revealed to you in open visions, you will hear the voice of God speaking to you directly (just as the Scriptures report), and often times you will know things that are just printed directly in your heart by the Holy Spirit – you will not be able to explain the source of this information.

Contrary to the prophetic anointing that works primarily for you, the gift of prophecy works for the Body of Christ. The gift of prophecy is a weapon, a dynamic tool; the Holy Spirit gives this gift to anyone He wants, especially to those prepared to serve the saints. The gift of prophecy does make you a prophet. It is a vital tool that equips you for service to the saints.

These are the basic signs that you carry a gift of prophecy

You experience the urge to see and speak about people's futures and to declare to them things that have not yet happened.

You will be able to hear the voice of God on behalf of other people and will be required to pass along the message.

You will have an open vision of things and they will be accurate, which sets vision apart from mere hallucination.

Your spiritual sense will be activated and will function just like your natural senses do. You will be able to hear, see, feel, smell and touch in the spiritual realm.

---

1 COR 12:7

But the manifestation of the Spirit is given to each one for the profit of *all*.

The Rise of the Prophetic Voice

> ### 1 COR 14:3
>
> But he who prophesies speaks edification and exhortation and comfort to men.

The prophetic call is different from the prophetic gift. A prophet is not one who operates with a prophetic anointing in his life that manifests from time to time; a prophet is also not someone who has a prophetic gift whereby God operates in his life. A prophet is one who is called into the prophetic ministry. The prophetic ministry is neither a gift of the Holy Spirit nor a simple anointing; it is a full-time ministry listed amongst the five-fold ministries.

A prophet is someone (a man or woman) called solely or primarily to serve God in the prophetic realm. The prophetic vocation is of a permanent nature and seems natural. All of a prophet's actions seem meaningful and have prophetic meaning.

With the gift of prophecy, it is as if you are someone carrying a gun; you do not have the gun – you are the gun. The prophet does not have a sign or a message. Rather, he is a sign, and he is the message.

Please note that there are no part-time prophets in this dispensation. Those called as prophets are called straight into full-time ministry. The demand in this ministry is so overwhelming that it is literally impossible to be a true and effective prophet on a part-time basis. Prophets are completely separated from others; they are sanctified unto the Lord. In the time of the Bible, we see that most prophets lived away from people; they have lived in mountains and out of the city. This is because to be a prophet you need to be permanently in the supernatural realm.

As a prophet, I have realised that a life of intensive prayer is the best oxygen for those called to be prophets. No other ministry has spiritual requirements like the ministry of the prophet.

Can You Ask God to Give You a Prophetic Anointing, a Gift or Call of God?

As a child of God, we can literally ask our heavenly Father to give us anything available to us in the kingdom. One can ask God to give the prophet the grace to operate in the prophetic either with a frequent prophetic anointing upon his life or with a dynamic prophetic gift to help him serve the Body of Christ. As for the prophetic call, I believe that one is born with that calling in one and it cannot be obtained through simple prayer.

> **JER 1:5**
>
> Before I formed you in the womb **I knew you;** Before you were born I sanctified you; I ordained you a prophet to the nations.

If you thirst to operate in the prophetic realm, either with the prophetic anointing or with the prophetic gift in you, you are to be applauded. Make sure you do so with faith and, since we are in a very strong prophetic season, a season where God is raising the prophetic voice across the world, the Holy Spirit of God will surely take you under His prophetic wings.

How Do You Maintain Yourself in Your Prophetic Assignment?

To be in the prophetic realm is a great thing, but maintaining yourself effectively in the prophetic realm has some rigid requirements. The worst in life is that *you are in the present but live in the past because you lost what you had.* Yesterday, you were dynamic in ministry but got distracted and lost your dynamism; today, all you speak about is yesterday. You speak about how you used to do this and that, how the Lord used you in this way and that way. You have clearly lost what you used to have, so now all you speak about is your yesterday.

I want to make this plea to you, as you are reading this book today, to please fight to maintain what the Lord has given you, and refuse to lose the anointing of the Lord upon your life. Please note that anyone standing can fall, so let those who think that they are standing take heed lest they should fall.

---

1 Cor 10:12

Therefore let him who thinks he stands take heed lest he fall.

Anyone who has received something significant from the Lord and who has been able to exploit it in the Lord can lose his anointing and become irrelevant in his work. If you operate in the prophetic realm, you must make sure that you maintain yourself in that grace and develop yourself in it. Timothy was told by Paul to stir up the gift of God that was in him. It is not enough to have the gift of God; you have to keep it working dynamically in you. God won't stir up His own gift in you for that is your sole responsibility.

> ## 2 Tim 1:6-7
>
> Therefore I remind you to stir up the gift of God which is in you through the laying on of my hands.

Anyone who operates in the prophetic needs to maintain himself in it. To do so, there are *four essential things to do:* 1. Grow in the knowledge of the Word of God; 2. Keep sharpening your beliefs in the supernatural; 3. Remain in the presence of God; 4. Sanctify yourself.

3. Grow in knowledge of the Word of God

The Bible is the written Word of God that has been given to us, the *logos* word, the open heart of God for His people, the will of God revealed. You cannot grow in the prophetic realm unless you grow in the knowledge of the written Word of God. Every prophetic word you receive or give has to be verified by the written Word of God. The prophetic cannot be in contradiction with the Word of God; on the contrary, it should be in confirmation of the Word of God.

A strong prophet is one who is strong in the knowledge of the written Word of God. Always remember that it is good to know His voice but it is always better to know His Word. In fact, I have discovered that the more you know the written Word of God, the more the prophetic ceiling is removed from above you. Therefore, it is critical that everyone who desires to maintain himself in the prophetic realm learn to study the Word of God.

Someone once told me, "I find it difficult to read the Bible because sometimes it is difficult to understand". I told him that, even when he feels that he does not understand some things in the Scripture, he must keep meditating and researching. The Holy Spirit is there

The Rise of the Prophetic Voice

to enlighten us through the Bible. *The more you open the Scriptures, the more the Scriptures will open to you.*

While growing in the Lord and taking baby steps in the preaching ministry, I remember that my pastor once obliged me to systematically read my Bible from Genesis to Revelation. This was in one of the prayer group meetings called *Les Pelerins* at our church in the Assemblies of God. I did it once and he said, "Do it again, and again, and again". I could not fully understand then how that advice would impact my prophetic ministry today, but I thank God that I obeyed my pastor.

JOHN 1:1-3

In the beginning was the Word, and the Word was with God, and the Word was God. He was in the beginning with God. All things were made through Him, and without Him nothing was made that was made.

JOHN 8:31-32

Then Jesus said to those Jews who believed Him, "If you abide in My word, you are My disciples indeed. And you shall know the truth, and the truth shall make you free."

---

4. Keep sharpening your beliefs in the supernatural

Believing in the supernatural is critical to the prophetic. It is impossible to be in the prophetic realm while being sceptical of the supernatural happenings of the Holy Spirit. Every prophet should be ready to accept and flow with the supernatural. To accept and to flow with the supernatural sounds easy, though it is by all accounts very complex; it requires that you let go of your mind completely and in faith embrace the works of the Holy Spirit.

No matter how hard we try to understand the works of the Holy Spirit in our lives, we will never be able to do so with our natural understanding. The things of the Spirit operate by different laws that are often completely contrary to our natural laws. Unless you give up the logic of our natural laws, you will never be able to make sense of the logic of the supernatural laws. It is simply impossible to do so. If your logic is based on our natural laws, it will be in complete conflict with the laws of the Spirit. Choose to operate and to flow on the supernatural level, irrespective of how intelligent you are. In fact, the more intelligent in the natural realm that you are, the more difficult it might become for you to understand the supernatural. To do so, your mind must be renewed (according to what is written in Rom 12:2).

Does this mean that we should not be intelligent or informed as far as the natural laws are concerned? No, it is good to be intelligent, but no amount of intelligence in the natural world will help you to understand the supernatural. This is why the Bible speaks of renewing our minds. A mind that is not renewed will not be useful in the supernatural realm.

> **ROM 12:2**
>
> And do not be conformed to this world, but be transformed by the renewing of your mind, that you may prove what *is* that good and acceptable and perfect will of God.

If, as a prophet, your faith in the supernatural starts getting weak, you will be the first to doubt the message of God to His people. You will start censoring every word that God has for His people to suit the acceptance level of your natural mind. Fear of being controversial may cause a prophet to become moderate with regard to the supernatural, thus compromising his prophetical stance. No matter how hard you try, all will not accept you, especially if you operate in the supernatural realm. Our Lord Jesus Christ Himself was controversial; the religious fellows of the time neither understood Him nor accepted His ministry. It is okay to be controversial at times; it is okay to be different. *Unless you accept being different, you might never make a difference.* Do not strive to fit in while God wants you to *stand out.* Keep sharpening your faith in the supernatural. Let your faith impose no limit on God and in return God will give your faith no limit. There is nothing God cannot do; give Him credit for His mighty works.

5. Remain in the presence of God

The strength of the prophetic dwells in the connection between God (the source) and the prophet (the conduit). As the prophet remains connected to God, he is able to be a dynamic conduit, a timely spokesperson and a powerful servant. Every great prophet reported in the Word of God was a man of prayer. Prayer is the most effective thing that allows us to tap into the presence of God and to remain in it.

If you are called in the prophetic and want to maintain yourself in it, you will have to be a man or a woman of prayer. Without a personal life of prayer, you will not be able to keep up in the prophetic realm; you will soon become ineffective and irrelevant. Prayer is so important that our Lord Jesus Christ Himself had a consistent life of prayer that was the greatest secret of His strength and earthly ministry. It was evident to those who were close to Him. So, His disciples asked Him to teach them how to pray.

> ### LUKE 11:1
>
> Now it came to pass, as He was praying in a certain place, when He ceased, that one of His disciples said to Him, "Lord, teach us to pray, as John also taught his disciples".

All the great prophets and prophetesses of God recorded in the Bible were men and women of prayer; and the Bible reveals to us their personal prayer. Prayer is indispensable to everyone that operates in the supernatural, especially in the prophetic. The more we pray, the more we connect with God, and the more we look like Him and are able to be like Him. Prayer does not change God; rather it changes us.

I learned to enjoy the presence of God immediately after I had given my life to Jesus and became born again. I remember that some friends and I would lock ourselves away for days, or even weeks, to seek the face of God. Today, spending hours on my knees in prayer before the Lord daily is like breathing for me. As I need air to breathe, I need prayer to survive. On a normal day, I spend a minimum of 8 hours on my knees in the presence of the Lord and much more when I go away on a prayer programme, which I do frequently.

To seek the face of God is better than to seek the hand of God. We seek the hand of God for intervention, but we seek His face for a relationship with Him. Many people today are often in search of the hand of God manifesting in their lives. Therefore, they enter into the presence of God with the sole purpose of asking for divine intervention on a matter. It is not bad to do so, but there is a level that is greater than just receiving from God. There, you seek God and do not merely grab whatever you can receive from Him.

Four young girls were once taken to a jewellery shop with an offer that whatever they wanted would be granted to them. It was a top- end, luxurious shop with the best jewellery ever seen by man or woman. They were obviously overjoyed by the rare offer and, in their excitement, they each began to look around for the jewellery of their choice. After a while, the man who had taken them to the shop with the offer to choose whatever they wanted, asked them whether they had made up their minds.

They first girl said, "Yes, I have chosen this exclusive set of diamonds". The second one pointed to the rare golden pieces inside a glass box. The third chose Tanzanite jewellery in front. To the astonishment of everyone present, the fourth girl remained silent throughout the time they were in the shop. She did not move up and down as the other three girls did, seeking out the best jewellery. She stood at the counter, immobilised. So, the man who had brought them there asked her specifically whether she was interested in any jewellery. He was ready to suggest that they might visit the next shop.

But before he could do so, the young girl asked him, "Sir, did you say we could choose anything we want in this shop and it shall be ours?" He replied, "Yes, anything," and jokingly added, "even the portrait on the wall". So, with a smile, the young girl said, "Well I know what I want". Since she was standing right by the counter, she pointed to the man on the other side of the table and said, "*I choose this man*".

They quickly told her, "No, this is the owner of the shop. You are meant to choose jewellery". She replied, "To me, this man is the best of all the jewellery I see here and, if I have him, I will have all the jewellery in this shop as well as him". The man who had brought them to the shop and everyone else present was filled with amazement and applauded her for her wise choice.

I love this story because it reminds me that those who run after *only* the blessings of God never get the better part of God, but those who run after God end up getting every other blessing that He has to offer.

To seek the face of God is better than to seek His hand.

If you are to maintain yourself in the prophetic realm, you have to learn to seek the face of God. Your relationship with God should not merely be in theory. Instead, it should be real through the intimacy you forge daily in being in His presence. You must have a structured and personal prayer life, without which you will neither maintain yourself in the prophetic nor be effective in it.

6. Sanctify yourself

The prophetic realm is so demanding that you will not be able to maintain yourself in it unless you cut yourself off from all distractions and attachments. To be sanctified means to be consecrated, dedicated, separated and set aside.

A prophet who does not understand separation will never be effective in the prophetic. The Scriptures often mention that most prophets live remotely or on their own. This is because prophets were not to entangle themselves with the affairs of life. Purity is one of the greatest parts of sanctification. Purity of heart and soul are indispensable for everyone who wants to remain effective in the prophetic realm. The prophet must live in a correct manner before the Lord and men.

Today, the emphasis in holiness is no longer on dwelling in a place of sanctification and holiness. It seems the revelation of grace has often been taken as licence to live sinfully. This struggle existed even in the time of the apostles. People have a tendency to accord themselves a licence to sin when it comes to the grace of God. In Romans 6, the apostle Paul clarified that being in grace does not imply that we can now sin.

> ### Rom 6:15
>
> What then? Shall we sin because we are not under law, but under grace? Certainly not!

The grace of God is not a licence to sin. We know that we are justified and it is true that our salvation does not depend on whether we have eaten and drunk or not. We are saved by grace and not by our works. This simply means that, once you have received Jesus Christ in your life, you have received your salvation and your place in heaven is secured. There are different views on whether, once you receive salvation, you might lose it again if you behave badly or contrary to what is written. I personally believe the belief that we could lose salvation belonged earlier to the Body of Christ, in the past when we did not know better. Our salvation is not linked to anything other than the presence of Jesus Christ in our lives, which gives us access to His saving grace.

> ### Eph 2:8-9
>
> For by grace you have been saved through faith, and that not of yourselves; it *is* the gift of God, not of works, lest anyone should boast.

We are *saved through faith, not of works.* But does this mean that sin is not a worry anymore and we can freely live in sin without any consequence? No, not at all: being saved by grace does not imply that we can live according to the gratification of our flesh, transgressing the commandments of God. Sin is dangerous; it has the ability to mess you up both physically and spiritually. It will destroy the course of your assignment on earth and weaken your inner being. If you want to maintain yourself in the prophetic and be effective in it, you must live a sanctified life away from sin. You cannot really be the voice of God if your life is not clean and you keep living your life in an ungodly manner.

A person given to excessive drinking, substance abuse, sexual immorality, unforgiveness, bitterness, hatred, gossip, envy and the like will not be effective in the prophetic realm – not because God is so disappointed in him or her that He has lost His love for them.

Rather a lawless life of sin will hinder people from connecting properly with God in the spiritual realm and will deter them from being able to do any godly spiritual work.

Live a life of sanctification and you will maintain yourself in the prophetic realm.

I would like to explore this concept of the CALL a bit more as it is crucial in assisting us to have a clear understanding of the prophet and the prophetic.

What is a Calling?

From the Greek

A calling is an authoritative command, spoken or written, to participate, to be present, or to take part in something, especially a summons to the hope of salvation in Jesus. The words "assigned" and "called" carry special weight because they imply that God exercises His authority in actively placing people where they are.

These concepts are sometimes used in non-biblical literature to mean "station in life, position, or vocation".

In the apostle Paul's literature, *klēsis* refers everywhere else to the call to salvation. In other words, God places us in various situations. We live out our salvation in the particular circumstances in which we are placed. The Greek terms *kalein, klētos, klēsis* are often used both in the Septuagint (i.e. the Greek translation of the Old Testament) and in the New Testament in the sense of calling, within mundane contexts: people are summoned to court and invited to dinner. But even in the Old Testament usage, the Hebrew *ḳara* or the Greek *kalein* have the meaning of calling someone, effectually for some purpose, which may signify "to call into existence".

Calling – Earthly

The concept points to the position in life occupied by each individual, and the duties towards society that pertain to such a position. These duties are primarily social rather than ethical, when performed for one's livelihood, and may be hedonistic (a hedonist is devoted to pleasure and can be self-centred). The theological idea of calling in the Bible is centred on the idea of God's summoning voice. God calls a people to be His own; this starts with God's call of Abraham, it is continued in His calling of the people of Israel, and it is now realised in His call to the church.

You must know your calling

God has created every one of us with a purpose; no one just happens to be born without a pre-arranged plan and mission of God. You were born with a calling by God in your life. You do not seek to have a calling; you already have the call of God and you should discover it.

> ### GAL 1:15
>
> But when it pleased God, who separated me from my mother's womb and called *me* through his grace

> ### JER 1:5
>
> Before I formed you in the womb, I knew you; Before you were born I sanctified you; I ordained you a prophet to the nations.

No one lands on earth by chance; with God, nothing "just happens". He has created every one of us for a purpose that is the essence of our calling. God carefully orchestrates all His creatures to fit into a specific place, in a specific time, and for a specific role. This plan is seen across nature: nothing exists without a purpose and the purpose of each one beautifully works in harmony with the purposes of others, like pieces of a puzzle. The ecological system is sustained by the participation of even the most unnoticeable bug in the forest. Thus, every creature and thing has a vital role to play because everyone is called for something significant.

A football coach does not position a player in the field to play a match without a clear role and expectation of his deliverables. In the same way, God would not deploy anyone on earth without a purpose, a role to play and a list of deliverables. Every football player placed on the field to play a match is called to contribute something vital to the success of his team; he is not expected to win the match by himself. But as he understands and plays his given role diligently, his team will stand a better chance to win. In the same way, God did not create and place us on earth – "our football field" – to play a match without giving us a specific role to play, which is our calling on the field.

Your calling cannot be upgraded

We live today in a very fast and dynamic society that keeps changing. Today, we are running at high speed, trying to cope with change and upgrades everyday. Everything around us is changing: our education system, our health, our politics, our mode of communication, and our way of exchanging and trading have all evolved a great deal, and they are still evolving.

Not long ago, we used VHS cassettes to watch movies; then we moved to VCD and DVDs. Now, all this technology is in the past and we have moved on to new things. Our television sets used to have large backs; we then moved on to using plasma TVs, and now our television is moving on to become an interactive laser television. Similarly, our medium of communication has evolved drastically from what it used to be. We upgraded from the sole use of the postal system for our letters to emails, Dropbox, WhatsApp, and so forth. We are no longer in the days of immobile telecommunication sets such as landlines; we have evolved to the era of mobile communication. We are now using cell phones, and so far the world has seen many different types.

Our society is not static. Everything around us is evolving rapidly and continuously. This affects our way of living and our way of being. It is now our mindset to look for the new, the upgraded version, "the better". The expectation of something new has come to the church of God also. We give our offerings to God electronically. Churches are making available to their congregations debit card facilities so that they may give unto the Lord. Announcements are done through multimedia systems, and special apps permit us to keep in touch with members of the congregation. More people now use Bible apps on their various devices instead of a good old book for the Bible. Most churches have taken down their signs that used to read: "Mobile phones must be off in the house of the Lord". People now use their mobile phones to read the Bible via their apps.

Though all this change is impressive, we have to know where to draw the line for upgrades. You can upgrade your lifestyle, your worship style, and even your preaching style, but you cannot upgrade your calling. The pressure of jumping from the old to the new is upon all of us, and because of it so many ministers feel bored in their callings. They want to move their callings to a higher level. Imagine a goalkeeper in a soccer match who feels that safe-guarding the goalpost is outdated for him and decides to upgrade his position in the match to be a mid-fielder or an attacker! What would the outcome for that match be?

Your God-given calling is for life and cannot be upgraded except by God himself.

You cannot change your calling

The same impulse toward a forever-evolving life has tempted many ministers to move on from their initial callings to something completely different, either to things on the list of the five-fold ministry or to something else. There are evangelists who decide unilaterally to become pastors. Then, there are pastors who decide to change their calling to become apostles, and so on. There are also some business people who are called by God to finance His kingdom as they travail in the marketplace. Then, these businessmen decide overnight that being in a full-time priesthood ministry is preferable and they abandon their initial calling to join the full-time ministry.

I know many a good man who is used by God to great effect. One of them had a great ministry, touching the lives of many in his country. He was well-known by all and highly respected; his reputation drew political leaders inhiscountrytoseek his advice and wisdom. He was seen as a father figure in his nation until he started contemplating the various possibilities that his influence could offer him and decided to run to be president of his country. He left his ministry, joined a political party, and he was quickly elected as a member of parliament, which sank his ministry. Slowly, the glamour of his honour in the country subsided to a normal level. Though he is still around, it is evident that this was a misstep and that he has lost his balance in life.

I am not implying that God cannot use a minister of the gospel in politics; I am merely affirming that you cannot change your calling. In this true story, the minister changed to become a politician. In the ancient world, people worked for a lifetime at the same job, but in today's world the average person is expected to change their careers at least four times.

The pressure of change is upon us. Though changing your career may not be fatal, changing your calling is. Remember, your career is an occupation undertaken for a period of your life with opportunities for progress, but your calling is the purpose of your existence, your vocation and life mission.

Most people are not given a sign from heaven as to what God wants them to do in life. Therefore, they have difficulty in truly knowing what their calling is. Some people of nomadic preferences have also not received their callings in life.

Eph 4:1

I, therefore, the prisoner of the Lord, beseech you to walk worthy of the calling with which you were called.

The Characteristics of the Calling

According to the Scriptures, God's calling in your life is holy, heavenly and upward.

It is a holy calling

> **2 TIM 1:9**
>
> Who has saved and called *us* with a holy calling, not according to our works, but according to His own purpose and grace which was given to us in Christ Jesus before time began.

The Greek of this text contains two active participles joined by "and" (*kai*). In Romans 8, the "calling" comes before the "saving". God's sovereignty (or election) is not at issue but, instead, "calling" refers to ministry ("called with a calling," cf. vv. 6–8). The New Testament language here is equivalent to the covenant language of the Old Testament (used in Israel). Believers in Jesus are the covenant people of God because they are called by God.

It is a heavenly calling

The *heavenly call* simply means the "call from God".

> **HEB 3:1**
>
> Therefore, holy brethren, partakers of the heavenly calling, consider the Apostle and High Priest of our confession, Christ Jesus.

The concept of *partakers of a heavenly calling* is used in several ways:

Israel was called by God to be a kingdom of priests and to bring the world back to God (see Gen 12:3, Exod 19:5). In the Old Testament, this was a call to service, not for individual salvation, but a corporate call to the nation of Israel so that Israel could carry out an assigned task, as a light to the nations (a kind of worldwide evangelisation).

Individual believers are called (John 6:44, 65) to an eternal salvation; every individual Christian is called to serve the Body of Christ through spiritual giftedness (see 1 Cor 12:7, 11).

It is an upward calling

Upward (ἄνω): at a position above another position, above, up.

PHIL 3:14

I press toward the goal for the prize of the upward call of God in Christ Jesus.

The upward call of God in Christ Jesus includes all the purposes that God has had in mind in saving us: salvation, conformity to Christ, joint-heirship with Him, a home in heaven and an infinite number of other spiritual blessings. This upward call includes the gifting that God has given to you.

CHAPTER FIVE

WHO IS A PROPHET?

> ### LUKE 7:12-16
>
> And when He came near the gate of the city, behold, a dead man was being carried out, the only son of his mother; and she was a widow. And a large crowd from the city was with her. When the Lord saw her, He had compassion on her and said to her, "Do not weep". Then He came and touched the open coffin, and those who carried *him* stood still. And He said, "Young man, I say to you, arise". So he who was dead sat up and began to speak. And He presented him to his mother. Then fear came upon all, and they glorified God, saying, "A great prophet has risen up among us"; and, "God has visited His people".

After witnessing the power of God, demonstrated by Jesus through a miracle that day, the people of Israel thanked God for raising a great prophet among them.

The people called Jesus Christ a *great* prophet. Prophets are not all on the same level. There are major prophets and minor prophets in the Body of Christ, great prophets and ordinary prophets. The level of a prophet is determined by the level of their service to the kingdom.

By raising a dead man to life, Jesus did the utmost service to the kingdom. Jesus restored life. Like Elijah, who also raised the dead, Jesus performed a sign indicating that He was a great prophet. More than that, He proved Himself to be the servant and agent of God, who alone has authority over life and death.

Israel thanked God because they understood the great benefit of having a prophet in their midst. If they had not known about prophets, and who they are, then they would have missed the signs of a prophet – nor would they have recognised Jesus Christ as a consummate prophet. If we know who a prophet is and the signs of a prophet, we will identify and accept him in accord with the Word of the Lord.

Foundational Thoughts

Prophets Are Neither Fortune-Tellers Nor Mediums

Though a prophet is able to reveal mysteries and to make predictions for the future, the prophet's role is not restricted to that of glimpsing the future. The prophetic ministry is far greater than that of a fortune-teller or a medium. In fact, fortune-telling and the practices of mediums are not godly; they are dangerous and evil. Those who practise them unknowingly invite evil spirits into their lives, which cause afflictions and oppression of all kinds. The operation of the prophetic is not to be confused with the deceptive work of a fortune-teller or medium. *A prophet does not sweet-talk crystal balls to gain a peek at the future or cajole spirits into revealing glimpses of impending events (which have not yet come to pass).*

Many times in my own ministry, I have sat with people whose sole intention in visiting me has been to gain special access and knowledge about the future, of the kind one might obtain from a fortune-teller or a medium. Their interest was to learn one or two

The Rise of the Prophetic Voice

specific things by way of foreknowledge; once they had heard what they had come for, they would leave – satisfied, as if such predictions about ordinary events were all they could expect to receive from a prophet.

How much wisdom, and benefit such people are missing! They behave as Nathanael did when Jesus rebuked him. Nathanael is impressed by the ability of Jesus to see him, sitting under a fig tree, by a sixth sense. Jesus rebukes Nathanel, "Because I said to you, 'I saw you under the fig tree,' do you believe? You will see greater things than these" (John 1:50). The things of God are the "greater things". Similarly, a prophet can predict events of the future sometimes; but how much greater are the things of God, which the prophet has to share.

Saul went to consult the prophet Samuel with the sole intention of learning the whereabouts of his father's lost donkeys. However, he got far more from his consultation than he bargained for. He encountered the true prophetic ministry of Samuel and he was anointed as the first king of Israel (1 Samuel 9).

There is a custom in the Body of Christ that if you are married to an apostle you automatically become a prophet or prophetess. Is a prophet merely the spouse of an apostle? No. A prophet who does not prophesy is not a prophet, just as a person who cannot cook cannot be called "a cook"; nor should a person who cannot drive be called a "driver". A prophet earns the name of "prophet" by functioning as a prophet. A prophet prophesies and, as discussed above, offers service to the kingdom of God by doing the life-giving works of God.

A Prophet Speaks on Behalf of God and in the Name Of God

A prophet is God's representative, who is anointed to speak on God's behalf and in His name. In the Bible, Prophets did not just report on the thoughts of God; they actually spoke the very words of God. For instance, the criteria of a true prophet from Deuteronomy 18 is that the prophet speaks the very words that God commands and only those words (Deut 18:18-20). Such a divine message may be a promise, a direction to take, an announcement of coming blessings, or sometimes a rebuke or a warning. The message that a prophet is given by God must be passed along accurately to the people. This message is called a prophecy.

One may wonder whether God still makes use of spokespersons to speak to His people, given that Jesus Christ has already reconciled us to the Father, and the Holy Spirit now guides us into all truth. Though it is true that we may be one with God through Christ, it is important to note that the church of Christ is not yet in a state of perfection. The Holy Spirit is still at work in the church to bring us to a place where we may be in fact blameless. To fulfil this assignment, the Lord our God has established men and women as His servants. They are to teach, strengthen, guide and build the church to perfection.

It can be extremely deceiving to reason that, because Christ has reconciled us with the Father, we do not need the ministry of men and women in our church. Christ did not come to remove the participation of godly men and women in our lives but rather to affirm and encourage that form of participation and service.

God has established men and women to speak His word to the church, to be His voice. Amongst those listed as part of the five-fold ministry, are the prophets. Prophets of God are not placed in the kingdom of God to be our *mediators* with God. Christ is the only mediator. Servants of God are planted in the kingdom of God to be *facilitators*: facilitators of the Word of God and of our growth in God. This is why we go to church and follow different teaching programmes. We have pastors and teachers to take care of us and to facilitate our spiritual growth. Again, it is dangerous and deceiving to believe that we do not need anyone to guide us since we have Christ as our mediator. We do need guides, teachers, prophets and servants who bring messages from God.

Any of us can hear God, but the ability to flow in the supernatural and to hear the voice of God is not natural, and not given automatically to people simply because they have given their life to our Lord Jesus Christ. God has anointed specific people, whom He has chosen and called, to be used in different assignments for our good.

Prophets are anointed to speak not only on behalf of God but also in the name of God. They are also able to speak words – under the prophetic anointing – into people's lives, into situations and circumstances in the name of the Lord. The words automatically bind as if they were from God Himself. This is the incredible yet threatening side of the prophets. Hence, a prophet in former times was called *man God* not *man of God.** People saw the prophet as *man God* because of the way he walked with God and operated under His authority and power amongst the people.

---

* Moses is called "man of God" (Deut 33:1; Josh 14:6; Ps 90:1; Ezra 3:2; 1 Chron 23:14; 2 Chron. 30:16). The concept of the "divine man" is much discussed in biblical scholarship. A classic study is by the German scholar Ludwig Bieler, *Theios Aner: Das Bilde Des "Gottlichen Menschen" in Wissenchaftliche Buchgesellschaft, 1967*
In the New Testament, the idea is traced to Greco-Roman ideas of divinity. See for instance, Erkki Koskenniemi, "Apollonius of Tyana: A Typical θεῖος ἀνήρ?," *Journal of Biblical Literature*, Vol. 117. 3 (Autumn, 1998), 455-467.

JOB 22:28

You will also declare a thing, and it will be established for you.

As this passage indicates, the prophet has the ability to declare something of his own initiative, without hearing it from God, and it shall come to pass. Elisha declared strong words to some boys who showed no reverence to him and mocked him because he was bald: bears came out of nowhere and punished them (2 Kgs 2:23-25). I am sure that God did not speak to him to curse those boys; out of his own heart and impulsivity, he spoke and the anointing in him executed his words.

Elijah called on fire to come down and consume the captain of fifty and his men. He said to them, "If I be a *man God* may fire come down and consume you". The Bible reports that fire literally came down and consumed them (2 Kings 1:9-14). What do you think happened here? Do you think that God spoke to His servant, the prophet Elijah, to call down fire on these men? No, God did not ask Elijah to call down fire upon them; that command was issued by Elijah himself as he wanted to demonstrate the power of God and to prove the authority of his identity in God.

These instances may seem to demonstrate that too much power is vested in a human being, and that is really what it is: too much power. The prophetic ministry carries so much power and authority on earth that an untrained, immature prophet may be more destructive in the kingdom of God than most demons.

A Prophet is a Person with the Spiritual Eyes Open

A prophet is a man or a woman of God whose supernatural eyes are opened. Prophets have the spiritual ability to see things beyond the natural realm, what a natural man or woman cannot discern.

> **1 SAM 9:9**
>
> Formerly in Israel, when a man went to inquire of God, he spoke thus: "Come, let us go to the seer"; for *he who is* now *called* a prophet was formerly called a seer.

The very term "prophet", amongst the people of antiquity, pointed to the ability that God gave to His servants (the prophets) to see beyond the natural realm. As God is once again raising prophets in our time, there are men and women with the ability to see beyond this material world. They are able to see what no eyes, x-rays, scanners, binoculars or microscopes can see.

> **NUM 24:3**
>
> Then he took up his oracle and said: "The utterance of Balaam the son of Beor, the utterance of the man whose eyes are opened".

This scripture speaks of the man whose *eyes are opened*. The open eyes in this scripture refer not to natural but to spiritual eyes. Just as a natural body has senses – eyes, ears, mouth, hands, nose – so our spiritual body has spiritual eyes, ears, mouth, hands and nose. Many people have their spiritual eyes closed to a certain degree, meaning that they are not able to make use of them to see into the spiritual realm. As Jesus remarked, "Having eyes, do you not see? And having ears, do you not hear?" (Mk 8:18).

Sadly, the state of many children of God, right now in the Body of Christ, is one of lack in terms of the spiritual senses. Although those called to be prophets operate at a higher level, so that they may see into the spiritual realm, every child of God is also given the ability to see into the spiritual realm because we are all spiritual beings. This ability is currently a point of contention in the Body of Christ, especially amongst ministers. Some seem to think that such supernatural sight is too far-fetched to be a possibility in anyone's life or ministry. Not only can these critics not see into the spiritual realm but they deny that anyone can do so. So, when someone attests to such spiritual sight, they assume this power is counterfeit and comes from the Devil; it must be that magic and divination are responsible. This contention surely brings great sadness to the Holy Spirit. The Holy Spirit desires to help the church of God to open up the gifts of the Spirit, including spiritual sight. We undermine the Holy Spirit's ability to work through us today because of our quarrels.

---

2 KGS 6:15-17

And when the servant of the man of God arose early and went out, there was an army, surrounding the city with horses and chariots. And his servant said to him, "Alas, my master! What shall we do?" So he answered, "Do not fear, for those who *are* with us *are* more than those who *are* with them". And Elisha prayed, and said, "LORD, I pray, open his eyes that he may see". Then the LORD opened the eyes of the young man, and he saw. And behold, the mountain *was* full of horses and chariots of fire all around Elisha.

This scripture clearly portrays life in the spiritual realm. The servant of Elisha is not physically blind; he is able to see with his natural eyes that the Syrians have surrounded them. There is nothing visible to the natural eyes that he is unable to see; but though his natural eyes function perfectly, his spiritual eyes are closed. His reactions are based on natural sight alone. Many people's reactions are similarly restricted and confined to the natural realm. If they were able to see into the spiritual realm also, their very reactions would change completely.

The servant of Elisha says in fear, "Alas, master! What should we do now?" The man of God, the prophet, does not panic, because he is able to see beyond the servant's capacity. To address his servant's concern and fear, he prays that his spiritual eyes might also open and they do open. The Bible says that the servant of Elisha sees the mountain, full of horses and chariots of fire, all around him. Elisha is a prophet, and as a prophet his spiritual eyes are opened.

A Prophet Operates More as a Spirit Than as a Human

John 3:6

That which is born of the flesh is flesh, and that which is born of the Spirit is spirit.

Many interpret this scripture to say that whoever is born of the Holy Spirit is a spiritual being. He has a spirit in him that defines him. Though this understanding of the verse is true, it is limited. The fact that we have a spirit within us is not helpful, in any way whatsoever. What did Christ really want us to know?

Whatever is born of the Spirit is a spirit; this person operates like a spirit, and he is no longer limited by the mortal limitations of man. Spiritual persons can speak and understand the language of the Spirit; they operate like a spirit. The reason that Jesus could walk on water is because He operated on earth like a spirit. What limits men did not limit Him. I am not referring to His divinity but rather to the fact that, even as a man, Jesus operated as a spirit.

As a spirit, a prophet can be physically here while his spirit is somewhere else. This kind of feat of bilocation should not shock you; you do not need to be a witch to be able to do such things. You just need to be a spirit.

> ### 2 KINGS 5:25-26
>
> Now he went in and stood before his master. Elisha said to him, "Where *did you* go, Gehazi?" And he said, "Your servant did not go anywhere". Then he said to him, "Did not my heart go *with you* when the man turned back from his chariot to meet you? *Is it* time to receive clothing, olive groves and vineyards, sheep and oxen, male and female servants?"

The New Living Translation says (v.26):

> But Elisha asked him, "Don't you realise that I was there in spirit when Naaman stepped down from his chariot to meet you?"

Elisha says, "*I was there in spirit*". The Hebrew term *leb* in this verse means "heart" or "spirit". It can mean: *inner person, spirit, mind, will* or *heart*. In the ancient Near East, the heart was associated with comprehension, not emotion.

The above scripture (v 26) could accurately read like this: "Did not my inner being go with you?" Elisha had extrasensory perception. He was able to travel *in spirit* even though his body did not move. Elisha is not really asking his servant Gehazi a question but rather strongly affirming the fact that he was very well present and a witness to what had taken place. He deplored his selfish actions.

A prophet is given a unique and superior ability to perceive things in the spirit. He can move like a spirit and understand spiritual things with exactitude. Many people under great and devoted prophets often dream about these prophets. These dreams are not natural ones. In a natural dream, one may dream of a prophet because the subconscious reflects a person's preoccupations. If people spend their days thinking of their prophets, then their minds get overwhelmed and their concerns will appear in the form of dreams.

However, the biblical understanding of dreams is different. Only two spiritual causes can compel someone to dream of their prophet. First, divine causation: God wants to speak to someone directly and decides to make use of a familiar face, who will have credibility in one's life. God uses the face of your *man of God*, your prophet. Second, people see their prophets in their dreams because sometimes, when a true prophet is travailing in prayer before the Lord for you – or whenever, by the anointing on his life, he is arising to defend your cause – his very spirit may be projected to cover you in the spiritual realm. Now, through your dream, your spirit sees him and he tries to communicate to you through images and pictures in the form of dreams.

If you are a prophet reading this book, please try to ask people around you whether they have seen you in their dreams and what their experiences with you have been. I am sure that you yourself will be shocked.

A Prophet Is a Man Or Woman Able to Know Hidden Secrets

There are no secrets for a prophet. A prophet is able to see things that are hidden. Even God reveals His own secrets to His servant, the prophet.

> **Amos 3:7**
>
> Surely the Lord GOD does nothing, Unless He reveals His secret to His servants the prophets.

Think of this. If God Himself reveals His secrets to His servant, the prophet, how much more will He reveal once He reveals the secrets of life? I am always amazed when I read the many reports of the ministries of the prophets of the past: how they were used by God, how accurate they were, the obstacles they had to surmount, and how they walked with God, demonstrating His power.

Prophets in the Bible were able to know the secrets and hidden things. Here is a beautiful story (2 Kings 6) of how God used the prophet Elisha, who was able to reveal to the king of Israel the hidden strategies of his enemies.

Israel was in great conflict with Syria, and it seemed like the Syrians had a much stronger army. But though the Syrians had a greater and better army, they still could not have their way against Israel. Every time the king of Syria and his major war generals were in closed council to discuss plans against Israel, Elisha the prophet would know their plans from the spiritual realm and warn the king of Israel. So, all the plans of the Syrians were spoiled. This lack of privacy, and the devastation, frustrated the king of Syria so much that he was convinced that he had a traitor in his camp. So, he called an urgent council meeting with his generals and asked that the sell-out in his camp be revealed, but one of his servants told him that there was no traitor amongst them; their plans were spoiled because in Israel there was a prophet who revealed to the king of Israel the very plans discussed in his bedroom.

> ## 2 KGS 6:12
>
> And one of his servants said, "None, my lord, O King; but Elisha, the prophet who *is* in Israel, tells the king of Israel the words that you speak in your bedroom".

The prophet Elisha, residing in a different place, knew hidden secrets from the king. In today's Christianity, Elisha would be called a magician who uses divination to know hidden things. Our generation in the Body of Christ seems to have forgotten that God is greater than magicians, and His power far more than that of Satan himself. Through the power of God, the prophet Elisha was able to know hidden secrets of the King of Syria. Foreknowledge is an ability that God gives to His servants, the prophets.

Often, when I prophesy and reveal things that have been kept hidden in a person's life, which may be the cause of his pain, people look at me, wondering how I could possibly know such private things. The simple truth is that God gives a special grace to His prophets to do so. This gift is not because they are superior or special people but rather because they are His servants.

When Saul was looking for the whereabouts of his father's donkeys, he was told to consult the prophets because it was well known that prophets have the ability to know things that are not known to men, even hidden secrets and concealed locations.

> ## 1 SAM 9:6
>
> And he said to him, "Look now, *there is* in this city a man of God, and *he is* an honourable man; all that he says surely comes to pass. So let us go there; perhaps he can show us the way that we should go."

This ability is not a reward for the prophets but rather a tool given to them by God to assist them in doing what is expected of them. There are prophets who are not yet able to know secrets or hidden things, but that is not because they do not have that grace in them; it is rather because they might still be flexing their muscles in that area. If they keep building themselves up in the prophetic, they will surely mature in that grace and start seeing everything with clarity, even those things that are hidden.

A Prophet Sits in the Council Of God

JER 23:18-22

For who has stood in the counsel of the LORD, and has perceived and heard His word?
Who has marked His word and heard *it*?
Behold, a whirlwind of the LORD has gone forth in fury –
A violent whirlwind! It will fall violently on the head of the wicked. The anger of the LORD will not turn back
Until He has executed and performed the thoughts of His heart. In the latter days you will understand it perfectly. "I have not sent these prophets, yet they ran.
I have not spoken to them, yet they prophesied.
But if they had stood in My counsel,
And had caused My people to hear My words,
Then they would have turned them from their evil way And from the evil of their doings.

This verse speaks of *the counsel of God* and *those who have stood in My counsel*. This counsel also suggests that the Lord our God has a council, and His servants, the prophets, sit in that council. A council is an advisory, deliberative, administrative body of the people, formally constituted, which meets regularly. When Amos said that the Lord our God does nothing without revealing His secret to the prophet, he meant not only that the prophet gets revelations from God (about the things God chooses); the prophet is also given access to the secret things of God for His people. Thus, the prophet sits in His council for men and earthly affairs.

God has a council where He decides the affairs of the universe. A prophet, *depending on his level in God's realm*, will sit in the council to report to the people what has been decided there concerning them. How can they speak God's word when they have not stood in "the council of the Lord"? This council is mentioned several times in the Old Testament. It was widely believed in ancient Israel that God Himself presided over the heavenly council. Whatever was established or decided in that council affected their day-to-day lives. Jeremiah felt that a true prophet was actually one who had been admitted to the meeting of this council and had received messages from the Lord.

> ### 1 Kgs 22:19-22
>
> Then *Micaiah* said, "Therefore hear the word of the LORD: I saw the LORD sitting on His throne, and all the host of heaven standing by, on His right hand and His left. And the LORD said, "Who will persuade Ahab to go up, that he may fall at Ramoth Gilead?" So one spoke in this manner, and another spoke in that manner. Then a spirit came forward and stood

> before the LORD, and said, "I will persuade him". The LORD said to him, "In what way?" So he said, "I will go out and be a lying spirit in the mouth of his prophets". And the Lord said, "You shall persuade *him* and also prevail. Go out and do so."

> **Ps 82:1**
>
> God stands in the congregation of the mighty; He judges among the gods.

The gods to which the Bible here refers are not angels (angels are not referred to in the scriptures as gods), nor are they idols (for the Lord our God does not sit in the congregations of idols); they are the anointed of the Lord.

> **Ps 89:6-7**
>
> For who in the heavens can be compared to the LORD?
> *Who* among the sons of the mighty can be likened to the LORD?
> God is greatly to be feared in the assembly of the saints, And to be held in reverence by all *those* around him.

A Prophet Is Entrusted With Divine Secrets

A prophet does not just have the ability to know secrets and to see hidden things pertaining to people and life. Instead, God Himself entrusts him with divine secrets. There are things that are only revealed to the prophet. No matter how strong you may be in the Lord, or how long you have known God or walked with Him, unless you are a prophet you will not have access to this information. Just as every one of us in the Body of Christ is called differently and carries a specific anointing for our assignments, the anointing of the prophets gives them access to divine secrets.

> ### Amos 3:7
>
> Surely the LORD GOD does nothing, unless He reveals His secret to His servants the prophets.

This verse does not present us with a suggestion but rather a fact cast in stone; the Lord does nothing without revealing His secret to his servants, the prophets.

A secret is a piece of information that is only known by one person or a few people and should not be told to others. It is something that is not meant to be known or seen by others. God has secrets, kingdom secrets, deliberately kept from all except those to whom He chooses to reveal them, namely to His servants, the prophets. This does not imply that God loves His servants, the prophets, more than others. Rather, because of the anointing of His servants, the prophets, He shares with them deep and rare information of the kingdom.

> ### Gen 18:17
>
> And the LORD said: "Shall I hide from Abraham what I am doing?"

In the olden days, people and their kings consulted prophets so that they might understand hidden mysteries. They came to know that prophets enjoyed a preview of divine secrets.

A great level of responsibility and trust is required by God of His servants. Is it fair to say that access to divine secrets is exclusive to prophets only? No, I don't think so. God is supreme. He may reveal His secrets to whomever He wants. The norm for Him is that He will do so for His servants, the prophets. Should this benefit be a subject of envy and jealousy within the Body of Christ? No. On the contrary, knowing that they are anointed by God and entrusted with

His secrets, we should have reason for joy and celebration. We are one Body with many members, and each member has its defined role to play for the good of the entire Body.

> ## 1 COR 12:12-26
>
> For as the body is one and has many members, but all the members of that one body, being many, are one body, so also *is* Christ. For by one Spirit we were all baptised into one body
> – whether Jews or Greeks, whether slaves or free – and have all been made to drink into one Spirit. For in fact the body is not one member but many. If the foot should say, "Because I am not a hand, I am not of the body," is it therefore not of the body? If the whole body *were* an eye, where *would* be the hearing? If the whole *were* hearing, where *would be* the smelling? But now God has set the members, each one of them, in the body just as He pleased. And if they were all one member, where *would* the body *be*? But now indeed *there are* many members, yet one body. And the eye cannot say to the hand, "I have no need of you"; nor again the head to the feet, "I have no need of you". No, much rather, those members of the body which seem to be weaker are necessary. And those *members* of the body which we think to be less honourable, on these we bestow greater honour; and our unpresentable *parts* have greater modesty. But our presentable *parts* have no need. But God composed the body, having given greater honour to that *part* which lacks it that there should be no schism in the body, but *that* the members should have the same care for one another. And if one member suffers, all the members suffer with *it*; or if one member is honoured, all members rejoice with *it*. Now you are the body of Christ, and members individually.

There is to be *no schism* in the Body of Christ. Not everyone is called to be a pastor or a teacher. The Body of Christ has many members who should work together in harmony for the well-being of all.

A Prophet is a Deliverer

Hos 12:13

By a prophet the LORD brought Israel out of Egypt, And by a prophet he was preserved.

The prophetic ministry carries a unique anointing for the deliverance of God's people. When God delivers Israel from slavery, He does not raise an army but rather a prophet. The Bible reports that by a prophet Israel was delivered and by a prophet Israel was preserved.

One of the major reasons why the prophetic voice is often under so much attack in the world is because a city, a nation and a generation cannot remain in bondage when the prophetic is operational. So, to keep families in bondage, nations sow confusion and generations are deceived. The enemy will always fight the prophetic voice of God. Therefore, Beloved, I urge you in the Lord to be careful never to join in the stoning of a prophet. The world will stop at nothing, just so that they may punish the prophet, even dragging many ignorant people, or uninformed believers, into the fight.

Believers could be under the naïve impression that, by such actions, they may be standing up against wrongs in the Body of Christ, while not knowing that the devil has carefully crafted a plan to turn the church against its own prophets. When servants of God do wrong and abuse their God-given offices, the Bible tells us what to do to address these wrongs. None of the recommendations of God in addressing the wrongs of His servants include permission for openly insulting, humiliating, or putting up a fight against them.

No matter how wrong a servant of God is, when you start insulting, openly fighting and humiliating him, please know that you are inviting judgment into your own life. You may feel that you are doing right and that your actions are justified by their wrongs, but I promise you, you will not escape judgment by the One who has said in His Word:

> ### Ps 105:15
>
> Do not touch My anointed ones, And do My prophets no harm.

Notice that the Psalm does not say: "Do not touch them, when they are correct to your eyes, but touch them when they make mistakes".

> ### Rom 14:4
>
> Who are you to judge another's servant? To his own master he stands or falls. Indeed, he will be made to stand, for GOD is able to make him stand.

Do not fall into the trap of the enemy by becoming like a whip, an instrument against the prophetic in our generation. Should things be wrong in the Body of Christ, the Lord has made provision in the Scriptures to address them.

I am not asking you to turn a blind eye to the mistakes made in ministry by servants of God. Please note that God does not call His servants because of their perfection or their seeming ability never to fail. Servants of God are saved by grace like everyone else and have to work out their salvation, with fear and trembling.

Though they are called to be first examples for believers and to maintain a high moral standard, these good qualities are not factors in qualifying prophets for their calling. They need Jesus just as we do. Instead of waiting for their weaknesses to manifest so that we may stone them, I suggest that we pray for these servants and cover them with love so that they may be saved. Our holy motivations will bring glory to God and close the door on Satan, who seeks opportunities to bring down the entire church family. Satan is terrified of the prophetic voice of our generation. He knows that the prophetic will expose his deception and defeat his plan.

The prophetic anointing brings deliverance. I have personally witnessed how people's lives, which were bound for years, are liberated; families that were made slaves of witchcraft in the spiritual realm are set free through the prophetic anointing.

Not only was Moses used to deliver Israel from slavery to Egypt but God uses His servant, the prophet Elijah, to deliver Israel while they are captive to *Baal* through *Jezebel* (1 Kgs 18:20-40). Chaos reigned in Israel. The enemy of the Lord had taken over His land, and His people turned from God to the worship of a foreign god; the servants of the Lord and those who remained loyal to Him were brutally murdered. Darkness had taken over right from the top and no one was there to help.

It seemed that God's people were stolen from Him forever. This was a huge problem, so serious, in fact, that it threatened the very plan of God for our salvation as it tampered with the core intentions of God. What did God do to remedy this situation? He raised a prophet because prophets are deliverers. He raised Elijah, the prophet; Elijah brought the fire of God on Mount Carmel and ordered that the prophets of Baal be seized. He brought them to the Kishon River and slaughtered them there. So, the land was cleansed.

If you read this scripture carefully, you will notice that God spared the lives of a number of good men who had refused to bow before Baal. They were upright before the Lord and refused to compromise their worship of God. God preserved 7 000 of them.

Seven thousand is a huge number, enough to start a movement or a revolution. But, though they were righteous and godly, they were unable to change Israel. Israel was facing a dilemma, which could be resolved only by a different kind of anointing. The anointing for their deliverance would come only through a prophet – in this case, Elijah. Note that the spiritual battle was so severe that many prophets were casualties of war. The absence of the prophetic voice in the land made room for foreign gods.

Deliverance from Famine

2 Kgs 6:25-33; 2 Kgs 7:1-18

Elisha was used by God to deliver Israel from great economic calamity; people in the land of the Lord even turned to cannibalism. The situation in Israel was dire, with problems that had already defeated the greatest generals, the best economists, strategists, wise men, and even the king himself. Israel needed a prophet, and God used Elisha to switch on the light of prosperity again. It was supernaturally done so that the closest officer, on whose arm the king leaned, doubted that such a thing was even possible.

There are situations of bondage in life, among families, nations and even generations, which require nothing less than an intervention by a true prophet of God. Through the word of a true prophet of God in a nation, the Lord will deliver that nation from its calamities, provided that the people listen to and obey the voice of the Lord through the prophet.

When I look at the realities faced by our generation today, I am convinced beyond doubt that God has to restore the prophetic anointing in order to deliver His people. The enemy has orchestrated the worst kind of deception. People are enslaved by every kind of yoke and subjected to oppression. More than ever, the power of God has to be demonstrated through a strong prophetic anointing to bring the world back to the knowledge of God. If nothing is done to rescue the church of God urgently, we will self-destruct, to the amusement of the enemy.

Today, the people of God are more and more individualistic than ever, and in our individualism we attack each other brutally and mercilessly. We strive to save face to the world and so we publicly join hands with the world to expose, humiliate and destroy each other. Where are those who were meant to defend the weak in the kingdom? Instead of fighting each other, how about praying for each other?

The church is fighting against itself: one side feels it can survive without the other. The left side of the body thinks it will remain alive even if the right side of the body dies. Not only that, the church is on a course of self-destruction and has joined the growing scepticism towards manifestations of the power of God. Churches themselves launch vicious attacks to remove God from the lives of our generation.

The world is in despair. More and more, it is evident that the world is losing respect and consideration for the Lord our God. There have been so many aberrations in the church of God today that the world has lost drive and the genuine love with which to embrace God and be embraced by Him. The world is trying to be self-sufficient and independent of God. As the church, we are the only ones able to address the tough challenges of our generation; but if we are asleep or in self-destruct mode, living without the agenda of the kingdom, what will happen to this generation?

The church claims to know the Word of God but completely ignores the voice of God. We do not understand that the light of the Word is in the voice of God. The voice of God is the spoken word, the *rhema*, which is the prophetic revelation within the written words. The voice of God stands for the prophetic ministry. Jesus called John the Baptist the greatest of all prophets because he was the voice. John carried a prophetic assignment, which was to prepare the way for the Messiah, the Christ. We are to know the Word through the voice of God, not only through the writings.

JOHN 10:27

My sheep know My voice. I know them and they follow Me.

When you face a difficult choice and there is no clear black-and-white biblical direction on the matter, you need to hear the voice of God to lead you in the right direction so that you can make the correct choice. You may be faced with a choice about whom to marry between two good gentlemen. Both are born-again and part of the same church; you will surely not find a biblical verse to lead you. You need the voice of God to tell you exactly which is your God- given spouse.

A Prophet is God's Spokesperson

> ## 2 Kings 3:11-12
>
> But Jehoshaphat said: *"Is there* no prophet of the LORD here, that we may inquire of the LORD by him?" So, one of the servants of the king of Israel answered and said, "Elisha the son of Shaphat *is* here, who poured water on the hands of Elijah". And Jehoshaphat said, "The word of the Lord is with him". So, the king of Israel and Jehoshaphat and the king of Edom went down to him.

When Israel needed to consult God, they looked for a prophet because prophets were the mouthpiece of God, known to be God's representatives and spokespersons. A spokesperson is an authorised mouthpiece and agent, mandated to speak on behalf of another. Whatever a spokesperson says is believed to have come directly from the one who provided the mandate, whose views and positions directly bind the spokesperson. Hearing the spokesperson is as good as hearing the person whom he represents. The prophet's word is extremely valuable because it is the Word of God himself, *rhema,* the spoken word, not *logos,* the written word.

Logos refers, in this context, to the written Word of God, meaning the Bible. *Rhema* means the spoken Word of God, which often addresses us directly, concerning our past, present and future. Here is an example of *rhema.* The Holy Ghost may use a scripture to address you on a personal matter. That scripture becomes your *rhema* word. Not every revelation you may get in the spiritual realm is called *rhema,* but only those deriving from the *logos* word.

The Word of the Lord is in the mouth of His prophet. Whatever the prophet says can be interpreted as *"Thus says the Lord".* This is why the Bible encourages us to trust the prophets:

> ## 2 Chron 20:20
>
> So they rose early in the morning and went out into the Wilderness of Tekoa; and as they went out, Jehoshaphat stood and said, "Hear me, O Judah and you inhabitants of Jerusalem: Believe in the Lord your God, and you shall be established; believe His prophets, and you shall prosper".

This scripture makes clear that we are to believe the prophets of the Lord. For someone who thinks that Jesus Christ came to remove the role of men or human ministers, it is difficult to grasp the ongoing significance of prophets and teachers in our walk with God. Someone who thinks that Jesus Christ has already provided us a direct line to God by cutting out all the middleman may reason that prophets and teachers are no longer necessary. However, the truth is that Jesus Christ has equipped and anointed men and women, whom He has selected Himself, in order to help the church to reach maturity and to be perfected. These men and women are not mediators in the sense that Jesus is a mediator – and they are certainly not substitutes for Christ. They are established, rather, to assist in the work for the church that Christ has initiated and fulfilled.

Besides doubting the prophets and teachers in today's church because of the mediating function of Jesus Christ, others question whether prophets are necessary, given the importance of the Bible. People may ask themselves, "Does God still need a spokesperson in our own times, today, to speak to us, seeing that He has already given us His word, the Bible?" A simple reflection will decide this question about whether God needs a spokesperson or not. First ask yourself, "Does God speak to us only through His written word?" The obvious answer in reply is as follows: "No, God does not speak to us only through the written word, the Bible". The written word of God conveys the basic truths of our doctrine. The Bible provides

The Rise of the Prophetic Voice

the complete will of God that is revealed to us. The Bible is also the launching pad for understanding God, both His creation and His kingdom. But the truth is that it takes maturity, and much studying, to understand this very Bible, the written Word of God, which is why Christ has appointed teachers to the church.

Though we are now believers and the Spirit of the Lord is in us, we still need help in understanding God's very Word to us. The teacher of the Word does not interfere, of course, in our relationship with God, nor does the teacher take the place of the mediator of God, who is Jesus Christ. Rather, teachers and prophets are established and equipped by God to help us to understand His Word. Now, let us think about another point. Since God does communicate with us not only through the written Scriptures but also by His voice, we need to ask ourselves, "Do we all hear His voice as we are supposed to?"

Jesus Christ came to rebuild us directly by Himself, by giving us salvation and reconciling us, spiritually, with the Father. No one else's assistance is required. In order to build the church to maturity, however, men and women have been selected, whom He has equipped and to whom He has given abilities that are spiritually valuable and divinely guided.

The world does not know the voice of God, nor does everyone in the church understand or hear God's voice. To keep communications going, prophets are used as spokespersons to make the voice of God heard in the church and in this world.

The Operation of the Prophetic Ministry

> ### JOB 33:14-16
>
> For God may speak in one way or in another, *yet man* does not perceive it. In a dream, in a vision of the night, When deep sleep falls upon men, While slumbering on their beds. Then He opens the ears of men, And seals their instruction.

The Book of Job is the oldest book in the Bible, and the depths of the prophetic are amazing. Already in those days, it was revealed to Job that our God is a speaking God. Job says that God speaks (Job 33:14). This important truth bears repeating: Our God is a speaking God. Many in the world and even in the Body of Christ do not understand this fundamental truth. A great deal of confusion unsettles the church and those who serve God when it comes to the prophetic.

God speaks not only through the Scriptures. God speaks to us in many ways, including the use of audible speech. Just as a man speaks to another man in an audible voice, so God may speak sometimes. Again, I emphasise that the written Word remains the foundation of all truth in God for the kingdom. We do not add or remove from the Scriptures. What is written forms the parameters within the church, by which we hear and operate in God. It may be most accurate to speak of God's consistency across various modes of communication, including sacred scriptures and non-written revelations. A spoken word or inspired revelation ought to be consistent with God's Word in written form.

God wants to speak to every one of us, His children, and even to those who are not His children. The Scriptures show us that God spoke to kings who were not even godly, like the Pharaoh of Egypt, Nebuchadnezzar of Babylon, and others. The principle widely accepted amongst biblical scholars through which God speaks to unbelievers is that God leads them to salvation. It is believed that God has no other business communicating with unbelievers except when He wants to speak to them about repentance from their sins so that they may be saved. Saul, who later became Paul in the Bible, encountered Jesus Christ while he was on his way to Damascus to persecute believers. Jesus spoke to him directly for salvation (Acts 9:1-22).

In the Book of Revelation (Rev 3:20), the concept that God speaks to unbelievers for salvation is confirmed:

> Behold, I stand at the door and knock. If anyone hears My voice and opens the door, I will come in to him and dine with him, and he with Me.

Jesus stands at the door of our hearts and knocks through speaking to us. This verse refers to our Lord Jesus' call to salvation. He is knocking at the door of our hearts, the hearts of unbelievers, in order to allow Him to enter and to rule our lives as Lord and Saviour.

Even though it may be true that God speaks to unbelievers to lead them to salvation, it is important to keep in the back of our minds that God remains a sovereign God. God's ways are not our ways. We ought not to fall into a form of a legalism when it comes to this principle. God's speaking to unbelievers cannot be limited. God may speak as God likes and deems fit. God is not limited to what we, or theologians, define as a call for salvation. In His sovereignty and immense love, God can speak to all of us, believers and unbelievers, about everything and anything. Remember that God loves us all, and He created every one of us for His glory.

Unbelievers are not loved less than others. God brings His rain to both believers and unbelievers alike, and causes the sun to rise on both without discrimination. We were all once unbelievers, yet never empty of the Lord our God. In fact, in the Good Samaritan story, for instance, the supposed "unbeliever" proves to understand the things of God better than the so-called "believers" (Luke 10:25- 37).

> ### Rom 5:8
>
> But God demonstrates His own love toward us, in that while we were still sinners, Christ died for us.

God speaks to all and He speaks clearly. He speaks but often human beings, men and women, do not perceive it. The prophet Jeremiah understood this fact when he rebuked foolish people: "Who have eyes and see not, And who have ears and hear not" (Jer 5:21). Only those who have the right attunement to God have ears to hear. "If anyone has ears to hear, let him hear" (Mark 4:23).

God Speaks to the Prophet
Clearly and Directly

Hearing the voice of God should not seem like a lie unless you believe our God is a liar. It is amazing to be able to clearly hear the voice of God. While growing in the Lord, it had been a mystery that God was able to speak directly to me. I had accepted the idea that God was a speaking God, but it was still inconceivable that He could speak directly. I was taught that the only way to hear God is through reading the Bible. To hear His voice was a mystery.

My idea of a speaking God was merely that He speaks to us in a very indirect manner through what is written; His *speaking* was more symbolic than real. I remember that it was through an aunt of mine, Aunt Celine, that I learned more about God's ways of communicating directly to us. My aunt was attending a church where it was said that the pastor, a man widely called Papa Gaston, and the leaders of the church, were able to communicate with God directly through visions. It was reported that the pastor and his trained leaders in the church would see visions of things. This all sounded very strange to me and far-fetched; I did not know what to make of it.

One day, my Aunt Celine took me to her church. I was shocked. The pastor or prophet in the church was able to see things in the spiritual realm, concerning people who were attending the service, and his spiritual sight was accurate. I was very afraid that he would speak about my family or me. I was very young but fear came over me, in the shock of what was happening right in my presence. I knew that there was something invisible and mysterious happening in that place and my question was, "Could that be God?"

Many had branded the pastor of that church an actor who staged his visions and pretended they were coming from God; others had said he was using demonic powers to receive those visions and believed he operated with some spirit of divination. *It is unbelievable how unbelieving believers have become today.* Without much thinking, we attribute any manifestation of the supernatural to the devil as if he were mightier than God. The experience in my aunt's church impacted my life in a big way, although I did not really go back to that church. However, this church left an indelible mark on my heart so that I recognised a great mystery and plain truth. Our God is a speaking God, and He speaks to His children and servants clearly.

The first time that I clearly heard the voice of God, speaking to me directly, is memorable. I remember the day, the time and the occasion. Since that day, my spiritual ears have opened up more and more to hear God clearly. Today, I hear God's voice more clearly than I hear the voice of my own spouse. God speaks to me in many ways, especially through an audible voice, a vision, and sometimes through writings. In another book, *How to Hear His Voice*, I will detail how God concretely speaks to me. I believe that the book will serve to ignite the same grace in many people's lives.

Next time you come across someone who claims that God has spoken to him or her, do not dismiss the claim. Listen and examine the assertion, in light of the written Word, the Bible, in conjunction with prayer, to determine whether the message might have come from God or not. The apostles who wrote the epistles in the Bible belong to our very dispensation even still, and yet they spoke to God and He spoke to them.

The spoken Word, *rhema*, and the written Word, *logos*, are flip sides of the same valuable coin: the revelation of God to us, personally. How amazing!

How Does God Speak to the Prophets?

Please keep in mind that the prophetic ministry operates with three strategic gifts: the gifts of prophecy, the word of knowledge, and the word of wisdom. This understanding will help you greatly to understand how God speaks to the prophets. After an intensive study and the guidance of the Holy Spirit, I came to discover that there are six ways often used by God to speak to His servants, the prophets.

1. Vision and Dreams
2. Direct Talk Through an Audible Voice
3. Advance Intuition
4. Revelation

5. Prophetic Sensations and Feelings
6. Sudden Knowledge (you just know something)

These six ways are often used by God to speak to His servant, the prophet. Some prophets will tell you that God speaks to them more through visions, advance intuition and sensations, while others will tell you that God speaks to them more through sudden knowledge and revelations. In all cases, these six ways are amongst those most often used by God to speak to His servants, the prophets.

Vision and dreams

Visions are distinguished from dreams just as they are in daytime experiences; they occur while a person is awake. Throughout the Bible, visions and dreams are the primary means of divine communication, and they are often used by God in at least three ways as follows.

First, visions and dreams provide information. A number of individuals receive dreams or visions, which instruct them to do or to avoid specific things. Dreams and visions also provide insights into current affairs and may reveal future events.

Secondly, dreams and visions serve as a means by which God directs events involving His people or His kingdom. In the early church, God used dreams and visions to guide the advancement of the gospel to new people and places.

Thirdly, dreams and visions provide a means to guide kingdoms even under unbelieving kings, just as in the time of Joseph and Pharaoh, or Daniel and King Nebuchadnezzar of Babylon.

Visions

> ### Ps 89:19
>
> Then You spoke in a vision to Your holy one, and said: "I have given help to *one who is* mighty; I have exalted one chosen from the people".

This verse speaks of a *vision*. A vision is the faculty or state of being able to see. In a vision, the emphasis is typically on an object that is visualised or a scene or sequence of events that is enacted. Vision here is an audio-visual means of communication between a heavenly being and an earthly recipient. The terms used to designate vision in both the Old and New Testaments have to do with seeing or perceiving.

In the Old Testament, prophets were sometimes called *seers* because of their ability to see beyond the natural and the visible. The gift or ability to see was evidently part of the divinely bestowed equipment of a *man of God* or a *prophet of God*.

> ### Num 12:6
>
> Then He said, "Hear now My words: If there is a prophet among you *I*, the LORD, make Myself known to him in a vision; I speak to him in a dream."

> ### Gen 46:2
>
> Then God spoke to Israel in the visions of the night, and said: "Jacob, Jacob!" And he said, "Here I am".

Visions are often closely coupled with dreams. Both experiences are regarded as legitimate channels of divine revelation, although the

Old Testament attests that counterfeit claims concerning both can be made. But the mere fact that there are counterfeit versions of a thing should never cause an outright rejection of it, because the fake only exists where there is also an original. So, if there is a fake, there is definitely also an original. Please note that visions are not limited to revelations of hidden things but also encompass vivid apparitions of spiritual beings.

> ### LUKE 24:23
> When they did not find His body, they came saying that they had also seen a vision of angels who said He was alive.

> ### ACTS 26:19
> Therefore, King Agrippa, I was not disobedient to the heavenly vision.

> ### 2 COR 12:1
> It is doubtless not profitable for me to boast. I will come to visions and revelations of the Lord.

In my personal experience, I constantly see angels around me, whether I am alone or in a crowd. The vision of angels in my ministry enhances and affirms what I do. I never gamble my ways while ministering. I am always well-informed about my actions and I am accurately guided.

In some instances, a vision is an ecstatic experience involving translation to other places. For example, the ecstatic experience of Ezekiel and other prophets of the Old Testament are described in the Bible.

> So I went and hid it by the Euphrates as the LORD commanded me. Now it came to pass after many days that the LORD said to me: "Arise, go to the Euphrates, and take from there the sash which I commanded you to hide there". Then I went to the Euphrates and dug, and I took the sash from the place where I had hidden it; and there was the sash, ruined. It was profitable for nothing. Then the word of the LORD came to me, saying, "Thus, says the Lord: 'In this manner I will ruin the pride of Judah and the great pride of Jerusalem.'"

Other instances occur that have been called symbolical perception. In this case, a prophet sees an ordinary object, which is part of the natural world, but sees it with a heightened significance beyond the normal.

> ### AMOS 8:1-2
>
> Thus the LORD GOD showed me: Behold a basket of summer fruit. And He said, "Amos what do you see?" So, I said, "A basket of summer fruit".
> Then the LORD said to me: "The end has come upon My people Israel; I will not pass by them anymore".

> ### JER 1:11
>
> Moreover, the word of the LORD came to me, saying: "Jeremiah what do you see?" And I said, "I see a branch of an almond tree".

> ### JER 1:13
>
> And the word of the LORD came to me the second time, saying, "What do you see?" And I said, "I see a boiling pot, and it is facing away from the north".

In this kind of vision, the Spirit of the Lord will show you ordinary things, such as a car, a watch, or a knife and use them as symbols to reveal to you something spiritual or to give you a prophetic message for His people. This is to say that, in the prophetic, anything can be a tool of the Holy Spirit, so as to minister or to speak the Word to His servant the prophet.

Dreams

There are two kinds of dreams recorded in the Scriptures: natural dreams and spiritual dreams. Natural dreams consist of ordinary phenomena in which the sleeper *sees* a connected series of images, which correspond to events in everyday life. Natural dreams happen to everyone. A dream is a series of thoughts, images and sensations occurring in a person's mind during sleep.

ECCL 5:3

For a dream comes through much activity, and a fool's voice *is known* by *his* many words.

ECCL 5:7

For in the multitude of dreams and many words *there is* also vanity. But fear God.

The second kind of dream is spiritual; these are dreams of the kind recounted in the Bible. Spiritual dreams are dreams that communicate to the sleeper a direct message from God. The following scriptures contain such messages from God in dreams: Gen 40:9-17; 41:1-7; Gen 20:3-7; 1 Kgs 3:5-15; Matt 1:20-24. Such dreams do not derive from a series of human thoughts, images and sensations occurring in one's mind during sleep; they are messages and images deriving from spiritual sources, whether from God's Heaven or the devil's spiritual realm.

Not All Dreams Come From God

Through spiritual dreams, God speaks to His people. But through spiritual dreams, the devil may oppress his victims too, or send them threatening messages of pain and death. Nightmares are dreams of oppression, aroused by the enemy to intimidate someone. They are often signs of a spiritual reality in the person's life. For example, if you are bound spiritually, you might likely have dreams where you are locked up; you are bound or in a grave situation. Often, such dreams may reflect the current reality of your spiritual being.

Some people have strange sexual dreams that seem real. Though naturally it is possible to have sexual dreams or wet dreams, these strange sexual dreams go beyond what is natural. The frequency of such dreams and their nature are the very indications that they are dreams of spiritual yet diabolical origins. This kind of dream is a sign of grave spiritual bondage and oppression in that person's life. Such a person needs to engage in spiritual warfare and deliverance.

There are two types of spiritual dreams: godly and evil. Here, I will focus especially on godly ones, dreams that come from God, prophetic dreams. God uses dreams to speak to His people and to His servants.

Job 33:14-16

For God may speak in one way or in another, *yet man* does not perceive it. In a dream, in a vision of the night, when deep sleep falls upon men, while slumbering on their beds, then he opens the ears of men, and seals their instruction.

This verse clearly states the use of dreams as a mode of communication between God and His people. God speaks through dreams when deep sleep falls upon men.

Understanding this divine mode of communication will help you to be more attentive and prepared to hear God through your dreams. Before you sleep, you should ask God to speak to you during your sleep through a dream. Ask also that He may give you the grace to perceive the message. There are many confirmations in the Scriptures that God has communicated to His people and servants through dreams.

> ### 1 Sam 28:6
>
> And when Saul inquired of the Lord, the Lord did not answer him, either by dreams or by Urim or by the prophets.

> ### 1 Sam 28:15
>
> Now Samuel said to Saul, "Why have you disturbed me by bringing me up?" And Saul answered, "I am deeply distressed; for the Philistines make war against me and God has departed from me and does not answer me anymore, neither by prophets nor by dreams. Therefore, I have called you, that you may reveal to me what I should do."

Dreams have always fascinated people; the events experienced in dreams are often too vivid and real to be ignored. Ancient records of dreams focused on three main areas: religion, politics and personal destiny. Dreams in the area of *religion* called for piety and devotions to the gods. Dreams that were *political* supposedly forecast the outcome of battles and the destiny of nations. Dreams of a *personal* nature guided family decisions and presaged serious crises.

Dreams played an important role in the lives of God's people, as consistently reported in the Scriptures. Of the 116 references to dreams listed in *Young's Concordance*, 52 come from Genesis, during the early patriarchal period, and 29 from the apocalyptic book of Daniel. In reality, however, only 14 specific dreams are recorded in the Old Testament. Most of them are in Genesis and reflect God's direct revelation to the patriarchs.

The Old Testament understanding of dreams has significant features. Like the rest of the ancient world, the people of God believed that God communicated in dreams. Where God was the initiator of dreams, however, He gave revelatory dreams when, where and to whom He pleased.

God Uses Dreams in the Old Testament To Protect His Servants

GEN 20:3-7

But God came to Abimelech in a dream by night, and said to him, "Indeed you *are* a dead man because of the woman whom you have taken, for she *is* a man's wife". But Abimelech had not come near her; and he said, "Lord, will You slay a righteous nation also? Did he not say to me, 'She *is* my sister'? And she, even she herself said, 'He *is* my brother'. In the integrity of my heart and innocence of my hands I have done this. And God said to him in a dream, "Yes, I know that you did this in the integrity of your heart. For I also withheld you from sinning against Me; therefore, I did not let you touch her. Now therefore, restore the man's wife; for he *is* a prophet, and he will pray for you and you shall live. But if you do not restore *her*, know that you shall surely die, you and all who *are* yours."

In the New Testament, God instructs Joseph to run for safety to Egypt. The Lord appears *in a dream* to Joseph.

> ### MATT 2:13
>
> Now when they had departed, behold, an angel of the Lord appeared to Joseph in a dream, saying, "Arise, take the young Child and His mother, flee to Egypt, and stay there until I bring you word; for Herod will seek the young Child to destroy Him".

If everyone paid attention to their dreams, many would realise that God kindly warns us of things to come. Before someone dies in a family, God may speak through dreams to the sons and daughters in that family and, if they are prophetically awake, they will know that the dream is a call to intercede; they could engage in spiritual warfare to overturn the situation. Very unfortunately, many forget the dreams that they dream and remember them only after they hear of their fulfilment, but by then it is too late. I urge you, Beloved, to take seriously every dream you dream; if possible, write your dreams down and take time to seek the Holy Spirit to understand them.

God Uses Dreams To Provide For His Sons and Daughters

God may use dreams to lead His sons and daughters to a place of provision and abundance. David said in Psalm 23: "The LORD *is* my shepherd; I shall not want," and then he explains why he will not want, because, "He makes me to lie down in green pastures; He leads me beside the still waters" (vv.1-3). The Psalmist thereby claims that God leads him to a place of provision and abundance, but the question is, "How does God lead us to such a place? Is it just through reading the Scriptures?" Though meditation upon the book of the law will empower us to make ourselves successful, it is mainly through the prophetic that God leads us to the place of our divine provision.

Therefore, I boldly say that through the prophetic you will be able to beat poverty and bad luck, for God will always lead you just as He did in the past with His servants. It is prophetically that Elijah was led to a brook, and there he had water to drink and a raven brought him food daily. This is why the Bible says that believing the prophet will make you prosperous (2 Chron 20:20). Dreams were one of the basic ways that God led people in Scripture to prosperity.

In this passage from Genesis, Jacob is talking with Rachel and Leah about a dream from God, which led him to provision.

> ### Gen 31:10-13
>
> And it happened, at the time when the flocks conceived, that I lifted my eyes and saw in a dream, and behold, the rams which leaped upon the flocks *were* streaked, speckled, and grey-spotted. Then the Angel of God spoke to me in a dream, saying, "Jacob," and I said, "Here I am". And He said, "Lift your eyes now and see, all the rams which leap on the flocks *are* streaked, speckled, and grey-spotted; for I have seen all that Laban is doing to you. I *am* the God of Bethel, where you anointed the pillar *and* where you made a vow to Me. Now arise, get out of this land, and return to the land of your family."

God Uses Dreams To Show A Person's Future

> ### Gen 37:5-7
>
> Now Joseph had a dream, and he told *it* to his brothers; and they hated him even more. So he said to them, "Please hear this dream, which I have dreamed. There we were, binding sheaves in the field.

> Then behold, my sheaf arose and also stood upright; and indeed your sheaves stood all around and bowed down to my sheaf."

In this prophetic dream, Joseph sees his own future symbolised, in relation to his brothers. Similarly, dreams can symbolise our own futures.

Some people will tell you that they came to know their calling in life through a series of dreams. A gentleman told me that he kept having dreams that he was in remote places on the continent, speaking to different groups of people; sometimes he would dream that he was speaking through an interpreter. He was a medical student and his parents had a great plan for his life. They wished for him to finish his studies, open his own surgery practice, and become an affluent person in society.

He was brilliant and finished well to become a medical doctor, but he struggled to find a stable job. One day, he got a call that he had been recommended for a part-time job in an international organisation by one of his former lecturers. They had a vacancy for three months; one of their doctors could not make it due to an international trip he had been obliged to take, and they were in urgent need of a replacement for his or her period of absence. He took up the offer and joined that organisation. They sent him with a team of doctors without borders to work in the equatorial forest, to assist pygmy communities and other remote villages.

The day he got to the field and began to work, he remembered the continuous dreams he used to have about being in remote places and speaking to small groups of people and sometimes using an interpreter. He broke down in tears as he realised that that was what God had prepared for him. Suddenly, everything started making sense: he understood why his applications for different jobs had

The Rise of the Prophetic Voice

been turned down so many times and why God seemed to take to heart exactly what worried and most concerned him. He remained in that organisation, serving as a doctor; he received many awards and recognitions for his outstanding work around the world, even in war zones. His future had been long revealed to him in his dreams, although he did not perceive it at the time.

Do Not Forget Your Dreams

Forgetting your dreams does not make them go away or undermine their meaning in your life. Many people have dreams, but in the morning they cannot recall anything about them. Some may still feel the intensity of what their dream had been, but they are completely unable to recall anything about it. You wake up in the morning knowing that you had a weird dream but you just do not remember what that dream was all about, and often the thought of that forgotten dream troubles you throughout the day. A forgotten dream may be a dream with an important message.

In Daniel 2, the Bible speaks to us about a dream of King Nebuchadnezzar. What is interesting is that the king had a dream that deeply troubled him. So, he set out to understand its meaning from his subjects without revealing to them his actual dream.

DAN 2:2-3

Then the king gave the command to call the magicians, the astrologers, the sorcerers, and the Chaldeans to tell the king his dreams. So they came and stood before the king and the king said to them, "I have had a dream, and my spirit is anxious to know the dream".

There are two explanations of this story. The first explanation says that King Nebuchadnezzar has had a troublesome dream. He has decided to ask for an interpretation of it from his subjects without revealing to them his actual dream. It may be that the king, here, takes an extreme precaution so as not to be misled by a made-up interpretation offered by his subjects. He may want to test them, to be sure that they are spiritually awake enough to interpret a dream of evident spiritual significance.

The difficulty in this first explanation is that it would be out of character for the king to behave in such a way. It was a norm that every king would surround himself with men considered to have supernatural wisdom and power to assist the king in various matters, including the interpretation of dreams, spiritual messages and signs. For a king to withhold the very dream for which he is seeking understanding is improbable.

This explanation might be possible if the king intended maliciously to lay a trap for his subjects or to test their claims of wisdom. But, should this have been the case, the king would have merely threatened them with the consequences of their failure rather than motivating them with a reward for success in their dream interpretation. The king seems sincerely to desire an interpretation of his dream, for which he is willing to reward his subjects:

> ### DAN 2:6
> However, if you tell the dream and its interpretation, you shall receive from me gifts and great honour. Therefore tell me the dream and its interpretation.

The second explanation is that King Nebuchadnezzar had a dream, but once he awakened from his sleep he was unable to recall its details or to remember it. So, he summoned all his magicians, enchanters, sorcerers and astrologers so that they might reveal to him his forgotten dream and give him its interpretation. I subscribe to this explanation. It is more plausible, and many may relate to it due to their personal experiences.

Have you ever had a dream that you cannot remember in the morning, and throughout the day you try to focus your mind to remember it? This happens to many people; they forget the content of their dream that they had in their sleep. They can remember only that they have had a dream that might have had great meaning, but they cannot remember what the dream was about. Once awake, they are troubled by the fact that they cannot remember it, so they push themselves to try. They concentrate, hoping to find some clue. If they are Christians, at times they pray to God to help them to remember their dream and to give them its interpretation.

So, this explanation reveals that King Nebuchadnezzar understood a certain truth. To forget a dream does not reduce its impact in your life. A spiritual dream may be a divine message or a revelation of important matters; if you forget such a spiritual dream, nevertheless the message is unchanged and the revelation made through the dream is still real and pertinent to your life.

Two things are often the causes when people forget their dreams. The first thing that causes people to forget their dreams is their weak, natural mind, which diffuses the images from their spirit and even their subconscious (in the case of natural dreams). The second thing that causes people to forget their dreams is the work of the devil. You must understand that Satan does not want you to be informed, and as long as he keeps you from receiving a divine message or a revelation of important things in your life, he will manage to keep you in bondage. Satan will stop at nothing to confuse your mind so that you will not remember the contents of your dream.

If you dream and frequently forget your dreams, I want you to pray this simple prayer with me for God to enable you never more to forget your dreams:

> **Holy Spirit of God,**
> I thank You for living in me and leading me in all truth. I thank You for giving me the power to operate in the supernatural realm so that I may be a true witness of my Lord and Saviour, Jesus Christ. I hereby pray that You also give me the ability to remember every spiritual message and revelation I receive in my dreams. Give me a clear mind that never loses spiritual information. I receive today the anointing and supernatural ability to always remember my God-given dreams. I decree and declare that my mind will never forget a divine message or revelation communicated to me through dreams. I thank You, Holy Spirit, for answering my prayer and for making me able to always remember my dream. It is done. Amen

CHAPTER SIX

THE WORD OF WISDOM

The gift of words of wisdom is not to be confused with the wisdom given to every child of God, through the fear of the Lord and through petitions to God. Wisdom is the principal thing, and the Scriptures encourage us to strive for it.

> **PROV 4:7**
>
> Wisdom *is* the principal thing; *Therefore* get wisdom. And in all your getting, get understanding.

What is wisdom? Wisdom is the ability to use your knowledge and experience to make good decisions and judgments. Wisdom is not knowledge but the ability to apply knowledge correctly.

An old African man was known in his village as a very wise man. One day, as he was travelling from one hut to another, he met a young boy who doubted his wisdom and decided to put it to the test. The young boy had a little bird in his hand, so he hid the bird behind his back and told the wise old man, "Today, I want to test your wisdom and know for myself if you are what everyone in this village says you are". He carried on, saying, "I hold in my hand a bird." (His hand was behind his back.) "Please tell me if the bird is alive or dead."

The boy had planned to embarrass the old man. He had said to himself, "If he says that the bird is dead, I will pull my hand out and show a living bird, and if he says that the bird is alive, I will quickly break the bird's neck and present a dead bird".

Anyone facing such a dilemma would feel stuck between a rock and a hard place, but in all wisdom, the old man answered, "Young man, the life or the death of this little bird is in your hand." And he went on his way. Everyone who witnessed this test applauded and cheered for the wisdom of this old man.

The young boy then realised, *"Indeed, this man is full of wisdom"*.

Wisdom does not deal much with the *what* but rather with the *how*. The wisdom of God comes to us as we fear Him and also as we ask God to give it to us.

PROV 9:10

The fear of the LORD *is* the beginning of wisdom, And the knowledge of the Holy One *is* understanding.

JAMES 1:5

If any of you lacks wisdom, let him ask of God, who gives to all men liberally and without reproach, and it will be given to him.

Wisdom can make or break anyone's success on earth. Your degree of success in life is conditional on the level of your wisdom. Your life cannot bypass the level of your wisdom, meaning that if your level of wisdom is below twenty percent, your level of life cannot be above twenty percent.

It is important to specify that the wisdom referred to commonly in the Bible is different from the *word of wisdom*, mentioned in 1

Corinthians 12 as a gift of the Holy Spirit. The *word of wisdom* is a supernatural ability to know how to apply knowledge. It is divine wisdom at work in a person's life, to address a situation or some important matter. With the gift of the word of wisdom, a believer is able to operate with divine wisdom that surpasses every understanding.

The mind of the Holy Spirit is conveyed to the believers by the gift of the *word of wisdom*, to resolve even the most complex situations. In the life of the local church, there are times when important decisions need to be made concerning a course of action. Through the *word of wisdom*, guidance for such matters can be provided.

The *word of wisdom* makes known God's purposes to His people for specific situations. It is a supernatural utterance, disclosing the mind and the ways of God in dealing with and addressing matters at hand. This word of wisdom gives a supernatural ability to a person, who may then speak with divine insight, whether in solving a difficult problem, defending the faith, resolving conflicts, offering practical advice, or pleading one's case before hostile authorities.

Many in the Bible are reported to be wise, but only when you fully understand what the gift of the word of wisdom is all about will you be able to differentiate between normal godly wisdom and the gift of the *word of wisdom* in operation.

For example, when the apostles recommended that deacons be appointed to serve in church, these servants were to be designated as men of wisdom amongst others. Which wisdom were they referring to here? The gift of the *word of wisdom*? No, they were referring not to the gift of the Holy Spirit but rather to the godly wisdom that every child of God may have and grow into.

> ### ACTS 6:3-4
>
> Therefore, brethren, seek out from among you seven men of *good* reputation, full of the Holy Spirit and wisdom, whom we may appoint over this business; but we will give ourselves continually to prayer and to the ministry of the word.

The men chosen must be *full of wisdom*. But, when you read the same chapter later on, the Bible speaks of Stephen and says,

> ### ACTS 6:10
>
> And they were not able to resist the wisdom and the Spirit by which he spoke.

Here, people are drawn irresistibly to the *wisdom and Spirit* of Stephen. The Bible is referring to Stephen's gift of the Spirit (his *word of wisdom*). This is why even the greatest minds of that time that were opposing him, could not resist him, namely those from the Synagogue of the Freedmen, "Cyrenians, Alexandrians, and those from Cilicia and Asia" (Acts 6:9).

Solomon's Wisdom

Solomon's wisdom was a supernatural gift and not ordinary godly wisdom. In this passage (v 28), the *wisdom of God* is responsible for the king's just administration.

> ### 1 KGS 3:24-28
>
> Then the king said, "Bring me a sword". So they brought a sword before the king. And the king said, "Divide the living child in two,

and give half to one, and half to the other".

Then the woman whose son *was* **living spoke to the king, for she yearned with compassion for her son; and she said, "O my lord, give her the living child, and by no means kill him!"** But the other said, "Let him be neither mine nor yours, *but* **divide** *him*".

So the king answered and said, "Give the first woman the living child, and by no means kill him; she *is* **his mother".** And all Israel heard of the judgment which the king had rendered; and they feared the king, for they saw that the wisdom of God *was* **in him to administer justice.**

CHAPTER SEVEN

THE WORD OF KNOWLEDGE

The *word of knowledge* refers to a supernatural ability to receive information, pertaining to a person, thing or event. This *word of knowledge* is given for a specific purpose, usually having to do with an immediate need. Such information may pertain to past, present or future events.

In my walk with God in the prophetic, I came to appreciate how dynamic and effective the gift of *the word of knowledge* is in the kingdom of God. This gift is one of the most astonishing gifts in the Body of Christ. It reveals the presence of God in a great way and magnifies Him amongst His people. When the *word of knowledge* is being exercised, the atmosphere becomes electrified and people get goosebumps; the glory of God becomes so thick that you have the impression of being able to touch it physically. Men's secrets are revealed and they are led to repentance. Verse 14 of 1 Corinthians speaks of how secrets of the heart are revealed.

> **1 COR 14:25**
>
> And the secrets of his heart will be revealed.

The gift of the *word of knowledge* restores the fear of God in the church and, along with the gifts of healing and miracles, it proves the existence of God in the world, more than any other gift I know. It is such a strong gift that maturity is required for its right handling or else its carriers may become puffed up and fall into the trap of the enemy by thinking too highly of themselves. Many servants of God are intimidated by this gift operating in others, because it leaves them feeling that they do not walk with God in comparison with those who have the gift. Instead of earnestly desiring to operate in it, they attempt to discredit the *word of knowledge* as if it were a devilish work or an unnecessary manifestation of the supernatural.

Maybe, like me, you too have heard someone in ministry, or in the house of God, who attributes the gift of prophecy or the gift of the *word of knowledge* to the devil, saying, "It is with demonic powers that they prophesy". This suspicion is due to ignorance of the gifts of God, which are given for the edification of the Body of Christ. Gifts are not given so as to cause people to feel competition as if they might be overly impressed with the manifestation of these gifts, thus rendering the gifts of others unnecessary. The gift of the *word of knowledge* is given to servants of God by God to support and strengthen other spiritual gifts, not to contradict or weaken them. (Through the gift of the *word of knowledge*, other ministries and gifts should be strengthened, not weakened.)

I have heard believers and ministers alike blankly criticising the operation of the gift of the *word of knowledge*, branding it entirely a scam. They believe this gift is staged and not real. They do not believe that God can speak with such detail about others. The *word of knowledge* is an indispensable gift in the prophetic ministry. Without it, a prophet would not be as dynamic as he should be.

Many great prophets have operated effectively in the gift of the *word of knowledge*.

Samuel

The prophet Samuel was able to tell Saul that a missing donkey had been found. Through the supernatural gift of the *word of knowledge*, he imparted this information.

> ### 1 SAM 9:18-20
>
> Then Saul drew near to Samuel in the gate, and said, "Please tell me, where *is* the seer's house?" Samuel answered Saul and said, "I *am* the seer. Go up before me to the high place, for you shall eat with me today; and tomorrow I will let you go and will tell you all that *is* in your heart. But as for your donkeys that were lost three days ago, do not be anxious about them, for they have been found. And on whom *is* all the desire of Israel? *Is it* not on you and on all your father's house?"

Elisha

> ### 2 KGS 5:25-26
>
> Now he went in and stood before his master. Elisha said to him, "Where *did you go*, Gehazi?" And he said: "Your servant did not go anywhere". Then he said to him, "Did not my heart go *with you* when the man turned back from his chariot to meet you? *Is it* time to receive money and to receive clothing, olive groves and vineyards, sheep and oxen, male and female servants?"

Here, Elisha says, "Did not my heart go *with you*," showing that his heart understands another by intuitive and supernatural means.

> ### 2 Kgs 6:12
>
> And one of his servants said, "None, my lord, O king; but Elisha, the prophet who *is* in Israel, tells the king of Israel the words that you speak in your bedroom".

Elisha is able from afar to sense the words that the king is speaking privately.

Jesus Christ

Below are biblical verses showing how our Lord Jesus exercises the gift of the *word of knowledge*.

> ### Matt 9:4
>
> But Jesus, knowing their thoughts, said, "Why do you think evil in your hearts?"

Jesus has the capacity of *knowing their thoughts*.

> ### Matt 12:25
>
> But Jesus knew their thoughts, and said to them: "Every kingdom divided against itself is brought to desolation, and every city or house divided against itself will not stand".

Here, too, Jesus *knew their thoughts*.

> ### JOHN 1:48
>
> Nathanael said to Him, "How do You know me?" Jesus answered and said to him, "Before Philip called you, when you were under the fig tree, I saw you".

Here, Jesus has the gift of spiritual or telepathic sight.

> ### JOHN 4:16-18
>
> Jesus said to her, "Go, call your husband, and come here". The woman answered and said, "I have no husband". Jesus said to her, "You have well said, 'I have no husband,' for you have had five husbands, and the one whom you now have is not your husband; in that you spoke truly."

Here, Jesus knows personal information about the woman's marriages and affairs.

Peter

Peter, through the gift of the *word of knowledge*, was able to know what Ananias and his wife caucused about in secret and had hid from the church. Without the working of that gift, he would have not known it.

> ### ACTS 5:3-4
>
> But Peter said, "Ananias, why has Satan filled your heart to lie to the Holy Spirit and keep back *part* of the price of the land for yourself? While it remained, was it not your own? And after it was sold, was it not in your own control? Why have you conceived this thing in your heart? You have not lied to men but to God."

How To Recognise a True Prophet

As in any dynamic ministry in the Body of Christ, Satan has his acolytes disguised as servants of God. It is, therefore, important to know how to distinguish true servants of God from false. Firstly, allow me to emphasise the fact that, as much as there are false servants and prophets of God in the world, there are also genuine servants and prophets of God. If you have had a bad experience with a false prophet of God, you may have a tendency to paint every other prophet whom you come across with the same brush, but *one bad prophet* does not automatically translate into *all are bad prophets.* There are genuine prophets, operating in the Body of Christ in our time, with a mandate to bring about the glory of God in this world. They will be a blessing to you if you know how to identify them and distinguish them from the false ones.

Here are four ways to recognise if one is a true prophet of God

1. What is the spiritual state of the person?
2. Does he fear God and walk according to His word?
3. Who does he exalt?
4. Are his prophecies verifiable?

The spiritual state of the person

The first place to investigate whether a prophet is from God or not is the person's spiritual state. Is the person born-again or not? There may be some nuanced discussions of what it means, precisely, to be born again. Nevertheless, as a general rule, those who walk and serve God are born of the Spirit and born again. If you are not a born-again child of God, or if you are separated from the Spirit of God, you risk being, spiritually, as if dead. We become children of God, born of the Spirit, when we accept Jesus Christ as our personal Lord and Saviour. No one is by birth a *child of God*, meaning that no one is born as a child of God. We are born in sin and need the Saviour to rescue us from eternal fire and judgment.

JOHN 1:12

But as many received Him, to them He gave the right to become children of God, to those who believe in His name.

You may have come from a Christian family and have grown up in the church, but that does not make you a child of God. *A piece of wood in a river does not turn into a fish no matter how long it is in that river. A bicycle in a garage does not become a motorcar simply because it is in a garage. A person does not become a child God simply because he attends church.* You are expected to personally make the decision to receive Jesus in your heart and to follow Him.

ROM 3:23

For all have sinned and fall short of the glory of God.

If you are not born again, you are still considered a sinner and you cannot, in anyway whatsoever, represent God or speak on His behalf. A person claiming to serve God as a prophet, who has never received Jesus Christ in his life, is not to be received as a prophet. He is surely an imposter.

Some years back, I heard a great prophet from God who attracted many people to him because of the number of miracles that he performed. This man grew in popularity almost overnight. He was revered by many as a true prophet of God. What was strange with his ministry is that, though he spoke frequently about God, he never mentioned the name of Jesus Christ in his ministry. He was a ritualist, and he said that one day God appeared to him in a dream and gave him the power to start performing miracles. Since then he had stopped using traditional medicines and rituals to heal people; he started healing by the power of God. He read the Bible in his ministry but mainly the Old Testament since he identified himself more as a prophet of the old rather than the new covenant. He was not a born-again child of God and did not recognise Jesus Christ at all in his ministry. Yet, this man claimed to be a servant of God. He was an imposter.

A servant of God must first be a child of God, and that can only be possible if he receives Jesus Christ as his personal Lord and Saviour. Servants of God are all "gifts of Christ" to the church, which is His own body. If you are not in Christ, you are completely out of the Body and out of His kingdom.

Does he fear God and walk according to His Word?

It is important to note that even true servants of God may have some weakness in them. They may be seen falling, here and there. Our journey on earth is full of imperfection, but through the power of the Holy Ghost and the Word of the Lord daily, we should grow stronger and stronger.

Perfection is never a requirement for God in choosing His servants, so it should not be our expectation from servants of God. It is understandable that a lot more is required of servants of God than of ordinary children of God, but it is important to always remember that servants of God need salvation as much as you do; they are not superheroes or supernatural beings.

MATT 5:48

Therefore, you shall be perfect, just as your Father in heaven is perfect.

Our journey on earth is not a journey OF perfection but rather a journey TO perfection. We are all trying to reach perfection, but no one has yet arrived there. On this earth, no one will ever arrive at perfection. Having said this, though, one of the signs of a true prophet of God is that he fears God and walks according to His Word. This simply means that, though a true prophet of God may not be without fault, he lives a God-pleasing life to the best of his ability. He does not practise sin and if by accident he falls into sin he quickly pulls himself back up again.

Can one who is not perfect still live a God-fearing life? Yes. When you fear God and walk according to His word, your devotion and commitment to God will lead you to a life of holiness to His honour. You will make sure that you do not compromise your godly virtues.

There are people who practise sin, and they live their lives in a way that completely disregards God and his commandments. Their lives are simply in opposition to the Word of God. A pig and a lamb may both fall in mud, but once in the mud, the pig will comfortably start playing while the lamb will be miserable and fight to get out. A true prophet of God does not practise sin and, if he falls into sin, he quickly repents and gets back in line. He cannot be a fornicator, an adulterer, a drunkard, a smoker, a thief, a liar, a fraudster, a greedy man, a bitter person, envious, gossiping, disobedient or rebellious.

To get you to accept their sinful lifestyle during ministry, some false prophets say, "Do what I tell you but not what I do". It is not possible to embrace this philosophy because your life is an integral part of your ministry. If you live in a wrong or sinful way, no matter what good you may speak about, your way of life will become a stumbling block.

You can tell people what you know but you can only give them what you have. If your spirit carries the seed of sexual immorality, no matter what you say against sexual immorality you will only produce sexually immoral people. They will take from what you carry, not from what you say.

Pure milk is good to drink, but if its container (glass) is dirty and infected, the milk will also be infected. So, do not drink milk from a contaminated glass. The milk here represents the Word and the glass represents the person who is being used as a container and vehicle of that Word. If the person carrying the Word is sinful and not aligned with God, then what comes from his or her mouth will be infected and will cause harm rather than good. A true prophet of God lives a God-fearing life and walks according to the Word of God. He is beyond reproach and carries a good reputation, both in society and in the church.

Who does he exalt?

A true prophet of God exalts Jesus Christ in everything he does. His work is to magnify the Lord and to place Him at the very centre of everything he does.

Satan was cast out of Heaven because of rebellion in his heart, which started with a great desire to claim the glory of God for himself. He wanted to become like God. His pride led him to seek self-exaltations rather them the exaltation of God. A true prophet of God carries the attitude of humility, as seen in the life of John the Baptist who said, *"He must increase, but I must decrease"* (John 3:30). He understood that the glory belonged not to him but to God.

False prophets use God's work for their own glory and self-enrichment; they make themselves the centre of their work and leave God out. They love big titles and recognition; their sermons are centred on themselves. They speak more about their possessions and their achievements than they do about God. A true prophet of God lives to glorify God; he exalts only Him. Through his work, the world comes to see not how great he is but rather how great God is.

Are his prophecies verifiable?

The words of a prophet should be verifiable; when they are not verifiable there is a loophole, which the enemy can use to deceive the people of God. When a true prophet speaks, his prophecies must be verified to prove that they are truly from God. When a prophet's prophecies are verified and proven to be from God, the prophet is confirmed to be genuinely a servant of God.

The words of the prophets are verified on two levels **and by** *two criteria:*

1. *Is his word aligned with the written Word of God (the Bible)?* Please remember that what is aligned with the Bible is not limited to what is written in the black and white printing of the Scriptures on the page. Rather, alignment refers to everything that is aligned with the Spirit of the Scriptures. There are many things that are not written in the Bible, yet

they are not anti-biblical. For example, the very word *Bible* is not found in any Scripture; yet we do not say that the *Bible* is not biblical.

2. *Do his prophetic words come to pass?* It is important that what a prophet says be taken seriously and watched carefully for its fulfilment. The prophet's words must come to pass unless such a word's fulfilment is dependent on the participation of its recipient. It is easy for anyone to claim to be speaking on behalf of God, but the fulfilment of the prophetic word is the greatest test of accuracy and genuineness for the prophet.

CHAPTER EIGHT

FALSE PROPHETS

> ### MATT 7:15
>
> Beware of false prophets, who come to you in sheep's clothing, but inwardly they are ravenous wolves.

The Bible speaks about false prophets and gives us ways to identify them. This chapter is important because it will give you vital tools to accurately identify the wolves in sheep's clothing around you and equip you with how best to handle them. In days such as these, where there is a clear revolution of the prophetic around the world, the enemy will also take advantage of the moment to infiltrate the Body of Christ. His own acolytes will deceive and destroy God's children.

Though false prophets have infiltrated the kingdom of God from the time of our fore-fathers, as attested in the Bible, I must say that there have never been such a great number of false prophets in history as there are today, and the number is still growing.

> ### MATT 24:11
>
> Then many false prophets will rise up and deceive many.

Our Lord Jesus Christ Himself warned us several times in the Scriptures about the coming of many false prophets; He said that false prophets would "rise". I believe He was specifically referring to this time: the era of the rise of the prophetic voice.

False prophets pose a serious problem in the kingdom of God. The potential destruction supersedes greatly that wrought by some of the best demons in Satan's service. Their terror today is at the core of the confusion that is now covering the Body of Christ and overshadowing the presence of genuine prophets of God in His kingdom. To be informed about false prophets will assist you in protecting yourself from their malicious and deceptive moves; you will be able to differentiate them from the genuine prophets of God. Consequently, you may keep feeding from the right source, from the prophetic. To reject every prophet and the prophetic move of God entirely, because of the presence of false prophets, is unwise and consistent with Satan's master plan.

How wise is it to stop using a currency because there are fake notes on the market? As much as there are fake notes, there are also genuine notes out there. Instead of punishing yourself by rejecting the use of bank notes, the wisest approach should be that you learn to differentiate the genuine from the fake and trade carefully.

How to Identify a False Prophet

Often, when the Bible speaks of a false prophet in the singular, it refers to a deceiver in association with an evil force. Revelation 19 speaks of the beast and the false prophet:

> ### Rev 19:20
> Then the beast was captured, and with him the false prophet who worked signs in his presence, by which he deceived those who received the mark of the beast and those who worshipped his image. These two were cast alive into the lake of fire burning with brimstone.

The Bible also speaks to us of other agents in the church and the world at large, to whom it refers as false prophets.

In Matthew 7, Jesus issues a warning about false prophets:

> ### MATT 7:15
>
> Beware of false prophets, who come to you in sheep's clothing, but inwardly they are ravenous wolves.

In the next verse, He provides a criterion for distinguishing the true from the false prophet:

> ### MATT 7:16
>
> You will know them by their fruits. Do men gather grapes from thorn bushes or figs from thistles?

Jesus gives this simple way for discerning prophets, to know if they are good or bad, genuine or false. He says we should observe them and consider their works or their fruits. This is the most practical technique for discovering the nature of a true or false prophet, but it is important to note that checking fruits is not the only way presented to us in the Scriptures as a means of discernment; it is the most practical touchstone, though, and one that everyone can apply. A true prophet will be like a good tree, bearing good fruit:

> ### MATT 7:17
>
> Even so, every good tree bears good fruit, but a bad tree bears bad fruit.

Before I give you a list of things that reveal false prophets, I would like to quickly speak about the three types of false prophets we currently have in the church and the world today.

Three Types Of False Prophets

Self-deceived

The first category of false prophets are self-deceived persons who desire to be prophets and who improvise themselves to be prophets. Though such an approach seems often to be innocent, it is nevertheless as dangerous as any other category of false prophets.

There are people who are so enthusiastic for the Lord that they want to push the kingdom of God forward by all means and often according to their self-will. In their enthusiasm and zeal for the kingdom, they run things themselves and do not wait for the Spirit of God to lead them. They give themselves titles in the church, and choose in which office or from what calling to operate. They speak their minds and opinions as the supreme Word of the Lord. They say God has spoken to them when God did not speak.

I heard of a woman who, on three different occasions, had dreams that she believes were very spiritual. In the quest to understand the dreams, she concluded that through them she had been called to be a prophetess. She believed it so much that no one could persuade her otherwise. She then proclaimed herself a prophetess and began to introduce herself as such. She is running a prophetic ministry, where her opinions are presented to people as prophetic messages from God. If she thinks that a specific brother should marry a specific sister in the church, not minding whether each of them might be already engaged in a relationship with someone else, she calls the brother and the sister together and tells them that God says they should be together and get married. Disobeying her words is like disobeying a direct instruction from God. She has been the cause of many scandals in the kingdom of God. She is causing a lot of pain in families with her misleading prophecies; she has made people quit their jobs to join the full-time ministry. The things she advised do not work out because there have been no instructions from God to back up her counsel. People have even died, as she has prevented them from going to a hospital or consulting a doctor, and all this is done in the name of the Lord.

There are many deceptive people who currently operate in the church as false prophets, and they are very dangerous. The majority of them are born-again believers who are unbalanced, immature, ignorant and untrained about the things of God. You have probably heard of prophets leading people in church to do unbelievable things, such as to drink toxic chemical substances, eat dead or alive raw animals, handle venomous snakes or scorpions with unprotected hands in a church service, kiss strangers romantically during a church gathering, ostracise their own families by calling them all witches, and so forth. Such self-styled prophets are all over the globe, causing havoc in the church of God and bringing shame to the prophetic.

Mercenaries

A mercenary is a professional soldier, hired to serve in a foreign army with the primary goal of making money. A mercenary does not fight for a just cause but for personal profit. No matter the conflict, you can hire a mercenary to join you against your opponent in a war and, without questioning you, the mercenary will gladly assist, provided that he is well paid.

Like normal mercenaries, there are those who have joined the prophetic with the sole purpose of using it for their own personal gain. They are intentional in their goals and will stop at nothing to fulfil their mission. These prophets are liars, thieves and manipulators; they are extremely malicious in their approach. They do not serve God and they have no love for the people of God. They are selfish, and they only run after what they can get. They are driven by their selfish ambitions to acquire more and more wealth for themselves. To seduce their audiences, these false prophets stage revelations and miracles, give false prophecies and manipulate people with dangerous tricks. Beware of them.

Infiltrated agents

This is a category of prophets who are acolytes of Satan and have infiltrated the Body of Christ, pretending to be prophets of the Lord. They have supernatural powers and can do wonders, but the source of their powers is Satan. Their main objective is not to be rich or to acquire wealth but rather to steal, to kill, and to destroy the children of God (John 10:10). Their targets are individuals in particular, and the reign of God on earth in general. They fight the coming of the kingdom of God on earth. They try to thwart the command of God and to prevent the will of God from being done on earth as it is done in Heaven.

Their work aims at weakening believers, causing them to sleep spiritually so that they will be exposed to the various works of demons. They deliberately create blunders to bring judgment in the church and persecution upon all the prophets. They are what the Bible calls "wolves in sheep's clothing".

MATT 7:15

Beware of false prophets, who come to you in sheep's clothing, but inwardly they are ravenous wolves.

> ## 2 COR 11:14
>
> And no wonder! For Satan himself transforms himself into an angel of light.

This category of prophets is the most dangerous and destructive in the world today. Beware of them.

Now I want us to consider some evidence or fruits that will help us to identify a false prophet.

Signs and Things To Know About False Prophets

7. Not called or appointed by God

> ## EZEK 13:6-7
>
> "They have envisioned futility and false divination, saying, 'Thus says the Lord!' But the Lord has not sent them; yet they hope that the word may be confirmed. Have you not seen a futile vision, and have you not spoken false divination? You say, 'The Lord says,' but I have not spoken."

Here, the false prophet is the one whom the Lord has not truly sent. A true prophet of God is mandated by God Himself to speak on His behalf; he operates under the anointing of God to carry out His task. A self-established prophet in ministry, or one appointed by any person other than God Himself, is not a true prophet of God; he is a false prophet. Please remember that some false prophets are false because they have either called themselves into ministry or they have been called and mandated by Satan.

8. Does not hear God

> ### EZEK 13:1-7
>
> And the word of the Lord came to me, saying, "Son of man, prophesy against the prophets of Israel who prophesy, and say to those who prophesy out of their own heart, 'Hear the word of the Lord!' Thus says the Lord God: "Woe to the foolish prophets, who follow their own spirit and have seen nothing! O Israel, your prophets are like foxes in the deserts. You have not gone up into the gaps to build a wall for the house of Israel to stand in battle on the day of the Lord. They have envisioned futility and false divination, saying, 'Thus says the Lord!' But the Lord has not sent them; yet they hope that the word may be confirmed. Have you not seen a futile vision, and have you not spoken false divination? You say, 'The Lord says,' but I have not spoken."

Here, the false prophets are those who prophesy out of their own imaginations, rather than truly by hearing and speaking the Word of God. One of the most amazing abilities of a prophet is his ability to hear God and to see into the spiritual realm. Without the ability to hear God, a person cannot occupy the office of a prophet. If a prophet cannot hear God, on whose behalf will he be speaking? Certainly not on behalf of God, and that makes him a liar. He is a false prophet, and his prophecies are made up. A true prophet tells people what he hears from God, not what he thinks in his head or what he gets from a source other than God.

9. Works for his own stomach

> ### PHIL 3:19
>
> Whose end *is* destruction, whose god *is their* belly, and *whose* glory *is* in their shame who set their mind on earthly things.

False prophets can be easily seen in their ardent pursuit of material gain from the people they are meant to bless through their prophetic ministry. They manipulate others to gather more and more for themselves; they target those who have and neglect those who seemingly do not have. The Bible warns us of many of such kinds: their belly is their god. They think that in the multitude of their possessions, they will find peace.

It is true that the kingdom of God needs resources to sustain itself so that the church may do the work of God here on earth. The message of giving and of prosperity should not be a taboo in the church of our God. A lot needs to be done in the Body of Christ to break the poverty mentality, which the enemy has systematically built into the fibre of our very belief system. We need the doctrine of Christ to help us dispel the illicit celebration of lack and poverty in the church today. Poverty does not mean holiness and lack does not mean humility.

Children of God may prosper, I believe, and be in health, according to the Word of God. As long as it is well and properly earned, any child of God, including servants of God, can own anything that they can afford, be it properties, cars, yachts, jewellery, and so forth. So, to be prosperous and to live a comfortable life should not be construed as being materialistic or as the mark of a false prophet.

There is no shame in wealth and prosperity – quite the contrary. Nevertheless, showy displays of wealth and ostentatious boasting are clues to a flimsy character. The false prophet puts his own gain and reputation above the things of God, which (in the case of a true prophet) are given to him to do and to communicate.

False prophets serve not God but themselves. In everything they do, their main focus is on what they can get for themselves. They will stop at nothing, in order to empty your pockets for themselves. They lie, manipulate and break the laws of God just in order to get from the sheep of the Lord more and more for themselves. They find glory in what they have and love showing off their riches and honours, as if to say, "I own this and that. Therefore, respect me more, love me more, consider me more than you consider others." Beware of them!

10. Takes advantage of the weak and the vulnerable

> ### LUKE 20:47
>
> Beware of the scribes, who desire to go around in long robes, love greetings in the marketplaces, the best seats in the synagogues, and the best places at feasts, who devour widows' houses, and for a pretence make long prayers. These will receive greater condemnation.

Jesus Christ warned of the scribes who went about displaying false spirituality in public and robbed widows of their possessions and their houses. The scribes here represent servants of God, those appointed in the house of God to lead His people.

In our context, this hypocrisy characterises, specifically, false prophets. False prophets target the easy prey in society and in the church, such as those whose emotions blind them from a rightful judgment of things, or those who are desperate for a solution – any solution.

Someone died mysteriously in a certain family, leaving everyone in great shock and with many questions, without answers. In their pain, as they were trying to come to terms with the tragedy, they received a call from a prophet in the area who had heard of their ordeal. He told them that God had given him a word, instructing that the entire family had to come to him for prayer, because there was a spirit of death roaming around the family; if they did not come within a week, another person would die mysteriously. He told them also to raise a significant offering for their deliverance.

The poor family was shaken, and panicked when they heard that there was a spirit of death roaming around them, which could strike again within a week. They were ready to do anything that the prophet asked, as long as he could prevent that calamity. They did not want to take the chance of disobeying the prophet and of suffering the consequences.

I came to hear about the story and the Holy Spirit vividly told me that the prophet was just an opportunist, who did not hear from God. I told the family that no one would die that week and that there was no spirit of death roaming amongst them. We built them up on the Word of God and strengthened their faith. True to my words, no one else died and the Lord healed their wounds. The prophet who gave them the prophecy targeted them because he knew they were vulnerable because of their pain. He is a false prophet. Beware of him!

11. Their work does not glorify God

> ### Isa 42:8
> I *am* the Lord, that *is* My name; And My glory I will not give to another, nor My praise to carved images.

God created us for His glory and His glory alone. The main purpose of our lives is to give Him glory. Whoever tries to share the glory of God will not be pleasing to Him. A false prophet fights for a share of the glory of God. He wants to be applauded, to be recognised and honoured, so much so that he gives himself big titles and names; he covers himself with the splendour of whatever material things are offered. A false prophet wants the world to believe that he is incomparable in his gifting or anointing. He pretends to be closer to God than anyone else in the kingdom, so that you may think that he is a vice-regent of Jesus.

> ### Ps 115:1
>
> Not unto us, O Lord, not unto us, but to Your name give glory, because of Your mercy, because of Your truth.

The glory does not belong to us but to God. Trying to play a more important role than God Himself is out of sync with His will.

> ### John 3:30
>
> He must increase, but I *must* decrease.

John the Baptist understood the right role of the prophet. He voluntarily resolved to decrease so that Jesus might increase. John the Baptist was an older cousin of Jesus in the flesh; he is the one who baptised Jesus and introduced him officially to the public for ministry. He naturally had some recognition to claim, but he did not claim anything; he chose to give Jesus the pre-eminent place. John the Baptist demonstrated that he was a true prophet.

False prophets do not give glory: when they say, "Lord, I give you glory," it is generic and a simple pretence. False prophets do not know humility; they live for themselves and claim a share of the glory of God. Beware of them!

Do Prophetic Words Always Happen?

Yes and No, depending on the particular category of the prophetic word in question. I know that right now you may be wondering what

I mean by *Yes and No* and by the question of prophetic categories. You will wonder how you can know whether prophetic words do predict or give rise to events that happen in reality.

Every prophetic word is meant to happen (i.e. to predict or bring forth an event that comes true in reality). Since prophetic words are Words from God, we might expect all of them to predict or bring forth events that come true and happen automatically. However, I would like to help you to understand that that is not the case for all prophetic words. Now, allow me to give you a general synopsis of the different types of the prophetic that we have in the Holy Spirit, and then I will put these types into two categories.

There are eight important types of prophetic words seen in the Scriptures, operating in the Body of Christ: peremptory prophecy, directive prophecy, revealing prophecy, comforting prophecy, announcing prophecy, warning prophecy, sentencing prophecy and apocalyptic prophecy. Each type of prophecy may work alone, but several or all of the types are often seen working together in harmonious combinations. This means that in one prophetic ministration, two or more types of prophecies may work together; peremptory or directive prophecy may work with revealing prophecy or warning. There may be other combinations that work together, too.

Peremptory prophecy

The peremptory prophecy is a type of prophecy that dictates what it wants you to do and leaves no option for you but to obey it. Not obeying would cause the prophecy not to be fulfilled and there might be other possible consequences. Here, the prophet tells you *to do one thing or another*, or *to come here or go there*, or *to take this or that*. Once you receive such a prophetic word, you should obey it and do it without trying to discount or debate what is being commanded. Sometimes a prophetic instruction may really seem unattainable, impossible to obey or irrational, but you are expected in God to obey it anyway.

---

1 KGS 17:10-16

So he arose and went to Zarephath. And when he came to the gate of the city, indeed a widow *was* there gathering sticks. And he called to her and said, "Please bring me a little water in a cup, that I may drink". And as she was going to get *it*, he called to her and said, "Please bring me a morsel of bread in your hand". So she said, "As the Lord your God lives, I do not have bread, only a handful of flour in a bin, and a little oil in a jar; and see, I *am* gathering a couple of sticks that I may go in and prepare it for myself and my son, that we may eat it, and die." And Elijah said to her, "Do not fear; go *and* do as you have said, but make me a small cake from it first, and bring *it* to me; and afterward make *some* for yourself and your son. For thus says the Lord God of Israel: 'The bin of flour shall not be used up, nor shall the jar of oil run dry, until the day the Lord sends rain on the earth'." So she went away and did according to the word of Elijah; and she and he and her household ate for *many* days. The bin of flour was not used up, nor did the jar of oil run dry, according to the word of the Lord which He spoke by Elijah.

This passage of scripture provides an example of a *peremptory prophecy* given to the poor widow of Zarephath by the prophet Elijah. Elijah instructs her prophetically to bring him water in a time of drought when water is scarce. As the widow obeys and is on her way to bring him water, Elijah instructs her again to make him a cake. At that, the widow replies (v.12), "As the Lord your God lives, I do not have bread, only a handful of flour in a bin, and a little oil in a jar; and see, I am gathering a couple of sticks that I may go in and prepare it for myself and my son, that we may eat it, and die".

Because Elijah the prophet insists, she obeys and the word of the prophecy comes to pass in her life; there is a multiplication of supply in her house. They all have enough to eat throughout the drought, thanks to and according to the prophetic word of Elijah: "The bin of flour shall not be used up, nor shall the jar of oil run dry, until the day the Lord sent rain on the earth".

I often caution prophets that, whenever they think they have a peremptory prophecy for someone, they should make sure, beyond any doubt, that it is from God; if it is, they should make sure it is delivered with maturity and not mixed with personal input. If you are at the receiving end of a peremptory prophecy, please make sure that you examine what is said in prayer, so that the Holy Spirit with His anointing may guide you in all truth. If the instructive prophecy is from an unfamiliar prophet, whom you do not know too well, or from a prophet who may not be accountable for your life, then it is especially important that you consult your own *man of God* or a *man of God* who understands the prophetic, someone you trust who can verify whether the peremptory prophecy is scriptural and genuine or not.

Peremptory prophecies carry such authority that they leave us no choice but to obey them. Many false prophets have used this type of prophecy to manipulate and to rob people. They say, "God said: do this and that," while God in fact did not speak such things. Unaccountable prophets, with no firm address, who move from place to place prophesying to whomever cares to give them an ear are dangerous since they are likely to take no responsibility for their actions. They will tell you things about what the Lord has supposedly said, such as that you should empty your bank account or sell your belongings. What should you do with the money? You will be told that you should give the prophet the money and bring to the prophet all the proceeds from the sale. If you obey, then they will receive what you give them and disappear into thin air while you wait for the fulfilment of their false prophecy.

This kind of fraud should not, certainly, cause you to refuse a prophetic instruction or word from a prophet who may in fact be reliable, even though he is someone you do not know. Rather, you should be cautious, because you do not know the level of the prophet's integrity.

Here is an example of a prophetic instruction gone wrong. A successful young man in a church was trusted by his pastor, who took time to invest in him and to groom him systematically for ministry. The young man had been showing fruit, and his potential was great. One day, a prophet met with him and, seeing his potential and that he was strong financially, the prophet gave him a very irresponsible and false prophetic instruction. He told him, "God said your time in your church is now over. God wants you to move and to start your own ministry, for he wants to raise you up to a position even greater than that of your spiritual father. If you remain in the church where you are, you will miss your season in God."

Though taken by surprise, the young man accepted the word and left his church to start a ministry. His pastor tried by all means to talk him out of it, but what are the mere words of a pastor compared to the so-called word from God Himself? That young man went his way and started his ministry in accord with the prophetic instruction he had received. His ministry is not taking off, his reputation is at its lowest, he is discouraged, he has lost most of his possessions, and the weight of what he is going through is badly affecting his health. I am sure that he is regretting his move and he has probably realised by now that he was deceived. The prophet who gave him the instruction to leave his former church and to start his own is not taking any responsibility; he is not concerned for the young man's well-being. He has moved on to his next victim.

Please note that God often uses this type of the prophetic to release great blessings in His children's life and to deliver them. We should be obedient to God when we receive a prophetic instruction, so long as we know beyond any doubt that the prophecy has come from God. Note that every prophetic instruction obeyed paves the road for a new dimension of God's grace and instruction.

Directive prophecy

Here, God uses His servant, the prophet, to give us guidance and direction as to where to go or how to go about the things we face. It is seen in the Scriptures that kings have consulted prophets to know whether or not to go to war or about various matters of the kingdom, including the economy.

---

2 Kgs 3:11

But Jehoshaphat said, "*Is there* no prophet of the Lord here, that we may inquire of the Lord by him?" So one of the servants of the king of Israel answered and said, "Elisha the son of Shaphat *is* here, who poured water on the hands of Elijah".

Here, the kings of Israel, in Judah and Edom, find themselves between a rock and a hard place as they are going to battle against the King of Moab who has rebelled against Israel after the death of Ahab. They march against him through the wildness of Edom and get stuck on the way as they run out of water for their soldiers and their animals. So, Jehoshaphat, the King of Judah, asks if there is a prophet of the Lord, whom they could approach to inquire of Jehovah by him. The King of Judah knows that God can give them direction through His servant, the prophet. Therefore, he neither asks for the greatest strategist of the Lord nor for the best general of war, but rather for a prophet of God.

Individuals across time have also consulted prophets, in order to receive directive prophecies for their lives and about various matters of concern. With directive prophecies, God will always lead you to take the right decision for your life, and you will always come out of a situation victorious. The directive prophecy shows you the path that the Lord has for your life. In this prophecy, you come to know the will and plan of God for your life and His light on where to step next.

Revealing prophecy

One of the most astonishing abilities of the prophet is the ability to see into the invisible world, to hear in the spiritual realm, and to reveal hidden things. A revealing prophecy deals with hidden things of the past, present and future. Such prophecies are directly linked to the prophet's ability to see and to know the most hidden secrets of things.

Amos 3:7

Surely the LORD GOD does nothing, unless He reveals His secret to His servants the prophets.

Secrets are the domain of true prophets; even the Lord God Himself does nothing without revealing His secrets to His servant, the prophet.

---

2 Kgs 6:8-12

Now the king of Syria was making war against Israel; and he consulted with his servants, saying, "My camp *will* be in such and such a place". And the man of God sent to the king of Israel, saying, "Beware that you do not pass this place, for the Syrians are coming down there". Then the king of Israel sent *someone* to the place of which the man of God had told him. Thus he warned him, and he

---

> was watchful there, not just once or twice. Therefore the heart of the king of Syria was greatly troubled by this thing; and he called his servants and said to them, "Will you not show me, which of us *is* for the king of Israel?" And one of his servants said, "None, my lord, O king; but Elisha, the prophet who *is* in Israel, tells the king of Israel the words that you speak in your bedroom".

Here, Elisha the prophet can pick up, remotely, the words spoken by the king in private. This passage recounts one of my favourite stories in the ministry of the prophet Elisha. I have always been inspired that he could see so deeply with his spiritual eyes that distance imposed no barriers. He could hear the discussion of an adversary king with his generals, while they talked in that king's private chamber in his kingdom!

Remember that Elisha did not have the Spirit of the Lord inside of him; he operated with the Holy Spirit in him. As born-again children of God, we have the Holy Spirit of God dwelling inside us. Those called into the prophetic have more in terms of the Spirit than what Elisha had. Elisha received a double portion of the anointing and the power that was upon Elijah, his spiritual father. Yet, we have received the power and the Spirit that was in Jesus Christ, our Lord and Saviour.

Most of my prophecies are either completely based on this type or they have a great deal of this type of prophecy in them. Through the prophetic ability of the Lord, I am able to see hidden things and to reveal secrets of hearts and life. Through the revealing prophetic ability granted to me by the Lord, my ministry has been able to impact the lives of a great number of people in an extremely powerful way. A revealing prophecy will root out a hidden problem in a person's life or family, which may have been the cause of their calamities for generations. This revealing prophetic word can bring about an immediate deliverance.

> ### LUKE 2:34
>
> Behold, this *Child* is destined for the fall and rising of many in Israel, and for a sign which will be spoken against (yes,   a sword will pierce through your own soul also), that the thoughts of many hearts may be revealed.

This prophecy by Simeon occurs at the birth of Jesus. The prophecy is a mixed type. Simeon makes an *announcing prophecy,* since he announces the destiny of Jesus and the salvation of Israel through the birth of Jesus. He makes a *warning prophecy,* since he warns Mary, the mother of Jesus, of troubles to come. However, Simeon also makes a *revealing prophecy* by stating that through Jesus "the thoughts of many hearts may be revealed".

Comforting prophecy

A *comforting prophecy* is the prophetic word that the Lord gives us through His servant, the prophet, to restore our hope, to encourage us, and to give us strength to keep going.

> ### Ex 14:13
>
> And Moses said to the people, "Do not be afraid. Stand still, and see the salvation of the Lord, which He will accomplish for you today. For the Egyptians whom you see today, you shall see again no more forever."

Moses, being a prophet of the Lord, spoke forth to Israel prophetically that they should not be afraid because the Lord was about to bring them deliverance. The main cause of their fear would be completely eradicated. This prophetic word was just what Israel needed at that time. I can only imagine their relief and peace of mind, since they were now assured that God was about to show up for them. They were comforted by the prophetic word that they had received.

> ### JOSHUA 3:5
> And Joshua said to the people, "Sanctify yourselves, for tomorrow the Lord **will do wonders among you**".

Here, Joshua is able prophetically to announce the wonders that God will do among them. The prophetic word of the Lord for His people was to revive them. After the death of Moses, God raised Joshua up to lead His people to the promised land. This task was not an easy one for Joshua, who was the servant of Moses, but God promised to be with him as He had been with Moses. The people of Israel, however, were filled with uncertainty and hopelessness after the death of Moses, their deliverer.

In Joshua 3, the Bible tells us that Joshua had been getting them ready to cross to the promised land, the very land to which Moses had promised to lead them before he died, the very land that had devoured its inhabitants (so they had heard), the land defended by the giant sons of Anak. I can only imagine how terrified the children of Israel must have been, at that point, as they prepared to cross the River Jordan. Yes, they were probably excited that God had brought them so far and that His promise to them was about to be fulfilled, but they feared the thought of the unknown. "What will happen to us when we cross? Are we going to be crushed by the sons of Anak? Will God show up for us or abandon us to our own fate?" Amidst everything that could have been going through their minds, Joshua stood and gave them a *comforting prophetic word* that restored their faith and hope. Comforted, they were ready to possess the promised land.

Here is an example of comforting prophecy. A person is troubled because of his past mistakes and thinks that God will punish him and make him pay for his wrongs. He lives in guilt and condemnation. He has taken a back seat in life and in the kingdom of God, since he feels really unqualified to do anything for God. He meets with a prophet of God who does not know him and who has no knowledge of his life. The prophet prophesies to him that God sees no wrong in him. His past sins are washed away by the blood of Jesus. God's grace has qualified him for greatness. Wow! This prophecy will surely turn his life around and bring him out of the dark pit of guilt. He has received a *comforting prophecy*; his life will never be the same again. This story shows what a comforting prophecy looks like. This type of prophecy is more common in the church today than any other kind.

Announcing prophecy

The *announcing prophecy* is a predicting type that speaks forth what is yet to manifest. It announces the future with accuracy. In this type of prophecy, God uses His servant, the prophet, to foretell future events to His people. The message of such a prophecy is generally good and uplifting in nature, although at times these prophecies are simply revealing God's future plans.

Acts 1:9-12

Now when He had spoken these things, while they watched, He was taken up, and a cloud received Him out of their sight. And while they looked steadfastly toward heaven as He went up, behold, two men stood by them in white apparel, who also said, "Men of Galilee, why do you stand gazing up into heaven? This *same* **Jesus, who was taken up from you into heaven, will so come in like manner as you saw Him go into heaven.**"

The Rise of the Prophetic Voice

Here, the two messengers make a prophecy that Jesus will return again in the future. This prophecy is one of the most exciting announcements made in this dispensation; it is the announcement of the Second Coming of our Lord and Saviour, Jesus Christ. The source of this prophecy is somewhat unusual and unexpected. The Bible says, "While they looked steadfastly toward heaven as He went up, behold, two men stood by them in white apparel". Here, *two men stood by them in white apparel*. The question is, "Who are these two men in white apparel?" They are not counted amongst the disciples of our Lord Jesus; they are not mentioned in the Scriptures before this. They are not prophets of the Lord. So who are they?

The Bible indicates that they were angels of the Lord, manifested in human form to fulfil an assignment, which is to deliver the message of the Second Coming of our Lord. They were sent to tell God's people that "it is not over yet; he will come back". But this is not the first time that we see angels delivering an *announcing prophecy*.

LUKE 1:26-38

Now in the sixth month the angel Gabriel was sent by God to a city of Galilee named Nazareth, to a virgin betrothed to a man whose name was Joseph, of the house of David. The virgin's name *was* Mary. And having come in, the angel said to her, "Rejoice, highly favoured *one*, the Lord *is* with you;blessed *are* you among women!" But when she saw *him*, she was troubled at his saying, and considered what manner of greeting this was. Then the angel said to her, "Do not be afraid, Mary, for you have found favour with God. And behold, you will conceive in your womb and bring forth a Son, and shall call His name JESUS. He will be great, and will be called the Son of the Highest; and the Lord God will give Him the throne of His father David. And He will reign over the house of Jacob forever, and of His kingdom there will be no end." Then Mary said to the angel, "How can this be, since I do not know a man?" And the angel

---

> answered and said to her, "*The* Holy Spirit will come upon you, and
> the power of the Highest will overshadow you; therefore, also, that
> Holy One who is to be born will be called the Son of God. Now
> indeed, Elizabeth your relative has also conceived a son in her old
> age; and this is now the sixth month for her who was called barren.
> For with God nothing will be impossible."
> Then Mary said, "Behold the maidservant of the Lord! Let it be to
> me according to your word." And the angel departed from her.

Angel Gabriel, an angel of the Lord, is sent to announce to a virgin,
Mary, that she has been chosen to be the vessel through which the
Messiah will come into this world.

In the Gospel of Luke, the prophetess Anna thanks the Lord for the
redemption of Jerusalem upon witnessing the birth of Jesus (Luke
2:36-38). Here she announces a good and mighty thing.

Simeon, in the same passage, makes a prophetic speech through a
revelation by the Holy Spirit (2:26). He also heralds the salvation
that is coming to Israel through Jesus.

These announcements fall into the category of *announcing prophecies*.

Warning prophecy

The category that we call *warning prophecies* may express the Lord's
displeasure towards the actions and behaviour of His people or they
may alert the people of an eventual danger ahead of them. The
main aim of such a prophecy is to save God's people from an evident
danger or pain.

> ## ACTS 21:10-11
>
> And as we stayed many days, a certain prophet named Agabus came down from Judea. When he had come to us, he took Paul's belt, bound his *own* hands and feet, and said, "Thus says the Holy Spirit, 'So shall the Jews at Jerusalem bind the man who owns this belt, and deliver *him* into the hands of the Gentiles'".

Agabus makes a prophecy to Paul, regarding his martyrdom. Agabus was one of the New Testament prophets; he was given a prophetic word to warn Paul of what would be waiting for him on his next trip to Jerusalem. His prophecy was not a prophecy of good news. Instead, terror was awaiting the apostle in Jerusalem. Paul, through this prophecy, had the option of carrying on with his planned trip to Jerusalem, knowing what would happen to him there, or to change his plan and to spare himself the trouble. The Bible says he chose to go, while accepting that he would suffer greatly there. He was forewarned.

> ## EZEK 3:17-19
>
> Son of man, I have made you a watchman for the house of Israel; therefore hear a word from My mouth, and give them warning from Me: When I say to the wicked, "You shall surely die," and you give him no warning, nor speak to warn the wicked from his wicked way, to save his life, that same wicked man shall die in his iniquity; but his blood I will require at your hand. Yet, if you warn the wicked, and he does not turn from his wickedness, nor from his wicked way, he shall die in his iniquity; but you have delivered your soul.

God has established His servants, the prophets, by a general mandate, to be watchmen for His people and to warn them of their sins and the consequences. And He Himself warns the prophets, to hold the prophets personally accountable if they do not warn His people.

Here, the prophet's mission is to give *warning prophecies* to God's people.

---

2 Chron 36:15-16

And the LORD GOD of their fathers sent *warnings* to them by His messengers, rising up early and sending *them*, because He had compassion on His people and on His dwelling place.
But they mocked the messengers of God, despised His words, and scoffed at His prophets, until the wrath of the LORD arose against His people, till *there was* no remedy.

According to the above scriptures, God has sent His messengers, the prophets, to warn His people because He has had compassion for them. *Warning prophecies* are evidence of God's love and compassion for His people.

Sentencing prophecy

Once things have already been judged and condemned, the work of the prophet is to deliver that judgment by a *sentencing prophecy*.

---

1 Sam 15:23

For rebellion *is* as the sin of witchcraft, and stubbornness is as iniquity and idolatry. Because you have rejected the word of the LORD, He also has rejected you from *being* king.

Because of Saul's open disobedience of the commandment of the Lord, God rejected him as king of Israel and informed His servant, the prophet Samuel, of His verdict. Prophet Samuel then went to tell him the Lord's verdict about his case. Although he pleaded for mercy, his fate was sealed and the verdict was irrevocable. A sentencing prophecy speaks forth the judgment of the Lord upon a person, a people, a nation, a situation, or an event.

Apocalyptic prophecy

An *apocalyptic prophecy* deals specifically with end-time events. Both the Old and New Testament are filled with prophecies announcing the events of the last day and beyond. The last book of the Bible focuses explicitly on events at the end of time and beyond.

> ### MATT 24:24
>
> For false christs and false prophets will rise and show great signs and wonders to deceive, if possible, even the elect.

Jesus prophetically announces to us here what to expect at the end of time, foretelling that many will come in His name, but they will be false christs and false prophets. They will even have power to perform great signs to seduce the very elect of God.

> ### 2 TIM 3:1-5
>
> But know this, that in the last days perilous times will come: For men will be lovers of themselves, lovers of money, boasters, proud, blasphemers, disobedient to parents, unthankful, unholy, unloving, unforgiving, slanderers, without self-control, brutal, despisers of good, traitors, headstrong, haughty, lovers of pleasure rather than lovers of God, having a form of godliness but denying its power. And from such people turn away!

In the above scripture, the author of 2 Timothy, which is attributed to Paul, speaks prophetically about perilous times, which are imminent in the last days. This speech does not constitute a teaching or a preaching because he is not speaking of things he could have known about in any way other than through a revelation, delivered prophetically.

This prophecy is what is known as an *apocalyptic prophecy*. In the Old Testament, apocalyptic messages are delivered in codes and parables. Prophets appear to be speaking of current matters but they are merely using the present situation or form of events as signs or codes for delivering a deeper message, an *apocalyptic prophecy*.

Zech 14:6-10

It shall come to pass in that day that there will be no light; The lights will diminish. It shall be one day which is known to the Lord – neither day nor night. But at evening time it shall happen that it will be light. And in that day it shall be that living waters shall flow from Jerusalem, half of them toward the eastern sea and half of them toward the western sea; in both summer and winter it shall occur.

And the Lord shall be King over all the earth. In that day it shall be – "The Lord is one," and His name one.

All the land shall be turned into a plain from Geba to Rimmon south of Jerusalem. Jerusalem shall be raised up and inhabited in her place from Benjamin's Gate to the place of the First Gate and the Corner Gate, and from the Tower of Hananel to the king's winepresses.

Zechariah is speaking about the Day of the Lord; the Day the Lord will finally establish His reign in the world. Although the prophet's message seems to address current events and things that would happen in his own times, in fact the prophecy points to the last days and to the decisive Day of the Lord.

I have listed eight types of the prophetic, but all of these types fall, actually, into two broader categories of the prophetic: *established things* and *the principal plan of God*.

Established things

In this category, whatever is prophetically revealed or announced – no matter to which of the eight types it belongs – is already established and requires no input for its fulfilment. A prophetic word in this category will happen if it is established and sealed. If a prophet gives you a word under this category and it does not manifest, he either did not hear God correctly or he lied. He is a false prophet according to the Scriptures.

DEUT 18:22

When a prophet speaks in the name of the Lord, if the thing does not happen or come to pass, that is the thing which the Lord has not spoken; the prophet has spoken it presumptuously; you shall not be afraid of him.

Please allow me to caution you that prophets do make mistakes, and their mistakes should not imply automatically that they are false prophets. If what a prophet speaks never comes to pass, it is easy to categorise him as a false prophet. But if one normally speaks things that do come to pass, but he sometimes fails to hear or to deliver the message of God correctly, he is not a false prophet. Do not be too legalistic. Discern spiritually, to understand how to deal with such matters.

Prophet Elisha gave a prophetic word of abundance to the king of Israel in the time of a great and long economic crisis.

---

2 KGS 7:1

Then Elisha said, "Hear the word of the LORD. Thus says the LORD: 'Tomorrow about this time a seah of fine flour *shall be sold* for a shekel, and two seahs of barley for a shekel, at the gate of Samaria".

This prophecy falls into the category of *established thin*gs. Such a prophecy is bound to happen as it does not rely on outside input for its fulfilment but instead upon the faithfulness and power of God. Though an officer on whose hand the king leaned doubted that the prophecy would manifest, his scepticism and lack of faith were not able to stop its manifestation.

---

2 KGS 7:2

So an officer on whose hand the king leaned answered the man of God and said, "Look, if the LORD would make windows in heaven, could this thing be?" And he said, "In fact, you shall see it with your eyes, but you shall not eat of it".

If this prophetic word had not come to pass, it could have been because it might not have come from God and the prophet might have been a false prophet.

The principal plan of God

The prophecies in this category reveal God's plan for His people, but it takes their obedience to make the prophesied events come to pass. The prophecies received in this category may or may not happen; it all depends on the input of the recipients, to whom the prophecies are given. If the receiver of this prophecy obeys and applies the conditions for the prophecy, its manifestation will come to pass, but if he does not obey and apply the conditions for the prophecy, it will surely not come to pass.

When Elijah the prophet asked the widow of Zarephath to make him a cake, she answered that what she had left was only enough for her and her son to eat that day – only for them to die the next day. The prophet insisted and gave her a prophetic word that her household would have enough provisions for the three of them. She did not need to eat that day and die the next. With these words, she went on her way and did as the prophet instructed.

1 Kgs 17:13-14

And Elijah said to her, "Do not fear; go and do as you have said, but make me a small cake from it first, and bring it to me; and afterward make some for yourself and your son. For thus says the Lord God of Israel: 'The bin of flour shall not be used up, nor shall the jar of oil run dry, until the day the Lord sends rain on the earth'."

The fulfilment of this prophetic word depended on the widow's obedience. Had she decided not to do what the prophet had instructed her to do, she would have eaten with her son for a day, only to die the following day. Those who do not know how the prophetic operates could have pointed fingers of accusation at the prophet Elijah; they might have called him all sorts of names.

The truth is that this prophecy belongs to the category of the *principal plan of God*. It reveals what the Lord has planned for us, which we need to take hold of through our obedience.

CHAPTER NINE

RIGHT ATTITUDE
TOWARDS A PROPHET

Prophets are God's servants of the highest order. It is important to know how to handle them and what attitude to have towards them. In this chapter, I would like to assist you with practical and systematic knowledge about the attitude to have towards your prophet. I believe this knowledge will allow you to be a blessing to your prophet and also to be an eligible beneficiary of blessings from Him.

Listen to Your Prophet

> **DEUT 18:19**
>
> And it shall be *that* whoever will not hear My words, which He speaks in My name, I will require *it* of him.

A true prophet is an authorised mouthpiece of God who speaks words that come directly from God. He is anointed to speak on behalf of God and to represent Him amongst His people as an ambassador. It is true that every child of God is Christ's ambassador to the world (1 Corinthians 5:20), but servants of God are His ambassadors to the church on a different level and more so; they are the prophets. Below are five major guidelines about the right attitude to have towards your prophet and things to do for him.

Honour Your Prophet

Honour is one of the greatest laws that exists in the kingdom of God and the world. Most of the writings and commandments in the kingdom of God are founded on the law of honour. The very first commandment is a promise to honour. The entire offering and giving system of the church is based on the law of honour. To worship God is to honour Him, to give to God is to honour Him, to obey God is to honour Him, to bless God is to honour Him, and to serve God is to honour Him. Where honour is not present, God will not be present. God wants us to know Him and also to honour His servants.

The Letter of 1 Timothy, which is attributed to Paul, says that the elders who serve well are worthy of double honour:

---

1 Tim 5:17

Let the elders who rule well be counted worthy of double honour, especially those who labour in the word and doctrine.

If the elders are worthy of double honour, how much more are the prophets established by God to be His voice and to speak His words to His people? They are surely worthy of the same or a greater honour. God wants us to honour His servant, the prophet. Your attitude towards the prophet must be one of honour. Without an honouring attitude towards your prophet, you will never be able to receive the best of Him. *You will never access what you do not honour.* So, by honouring the prophet, you are in fact doing yourself a great favour and your life will be blessed.

To honour is to have high regard, high respect and great esteem. Honour is an attitude that should be demonstrated through words and actions. When you honour someone, you speak highly of them and you do so with great respect. You also express it with your actions towards them. Make sure that you act and speak with honour to and about your prophet.

Do Your Prophet No Harm

Prophets are often the targets of many attacks from the enemy. Not only are demons of all kinds deployed against them, but the devil raises many in the world and in the church against them. Some of those raised by the devil against the prophets are not even aware that they have been used by the devil. Satan is so deceptive that he makes them feel that they are standing for the right cause and they are serving God in attacking and harming prophets. They are meant to believe that prophets are fake; they regard prophets as manipulators, deceivers and people who should be dealt with.

> **Ps 105:14-15**
>
> He permitted no one to do them wrong; Yes, He rebuked kings for their sakes, *saying*, "Do not touch My anointed ones, And do My prophets no harm".

> **1 Chron 16:20-22**
>
> When they went from one nation to another, and from *one* kingdom to another people, He permitted no man to do them wrong; Yes, He rebuked kings for their sakes, *Saying*, "Do not touch My anointed ones, And do my prophets no harm."

God gives a direct command to everyone that His prophet should neither be touched nor harmed. It does not matter what issue you may have with His prophet, whether they are wrong and you are right; as long as they are His prophets, He has said, *"Touch not, harm not."* His Word says, "He permitted no man to do them wrong; Yes, he rebuked kings for their sakes." This point simply means that nothing before God justifies an attack on a true prophet of God. It really does not matter what the issue is: if he has done you wrong, let God Himself be the One to handle it and, believe me, God knows how to handle His own servants. The Bible says that God killed Moses but He did not permit his own sister Miriam to harm him.

NUM 12:1-5

Then Miriam and Aaron spoke against Moses because of the Ethiopian woman whom he had married; for he had married an Ethiopian woman. So they said, "Has the LORD indeed spoken only through Moses? Has He not spoken through us also?" And the LORD heard *it*. (Now the man Moses was very humble, more than all men who were on the face of the earth.)
Suddenly the LORD said to Moses, Aaron, and Miriam, "Come out, you three, to the tabernacle of meeting!" So the three came out. Then the LORD came down in the pillar of cloud and stood *in* the door of the tabernacle, and called Aaron and Miriam. And they both went forward.

NUM 12:9-10

So the anger of the LORD was aroused against them, and He departed. And when the cloud departed from above the tabernacle, suddenly Miriam *became* leprous, as *white* as snow. Then Aaron turned toward Miriam, and there she was, a leper.

In this story, Miriam complains that Moses, the leader and prophet over Israel, is not living according to his own preaching because he has married a foreigner, a gorgeous African woman from Ethiopia. So, she questions the spiritual position of Moses as a prophet over Israel: "Has

The Rise of the Prophetic Voice

the Lord spoken *only* through Moses? Has He not also spoken through us?" It was clear to mere men that she had a point; Moses told Israel not to marry foreigners but he himself had an African beauty as a wife.

> ## DEUT 7:3
>
> Nor shall you make marriages with them. You shall not give your daughter to their son, nor take their daughter for your son.

> ## 1 KGS 11:2
>
> They were from the nations of whom the LORD had said to the children of Israel, "You shall not intermarry with them, nor they with you. Surely they will turn away your hearts after their gods." Solomon clung to these in love.

According to the law, Moses was wrong and Miriam could have appeared as a concerned, righteous person, who was sincerely trying to straighten things that had gone terribly wrong, at the very top of the leadership of Israel. What she did not understand is that this kind of correction is something that God would not allow one to do to His prophet, no matter what. Unless you are dealing with a false prophet, there will be severe consequences for you. You must not touch, by mistake or by will, a true prophet of God.

The actions of Miriam displeased God so much that the Bible says, "The anger of the LORD was aroused against them, and He departed" (Num 12:9). And that is simply because God does not permit anyone to touch or to harm His prophets. It is even said that He rebuked kings for their sakes, meaning that even kings will face God if they dare to touch or to harm His prophets. If kings would face the wrath of God because of the prophets, you should understand how serious this matter is to the Lord.

Please note that I am not here elevating prophets to the level of faultless beings who are always right in all their doings. Prophets are not chosen by God because of their perfection; they are sinners saved by grace like everyone else, and they apply the Word of God in their lives, every day, to be more like Christ. What I am saying here is that, even in their imperfections and the mistakes of their lives, God does not permit you to be their prosecutors and to harm them. He holds the exclusive right over them. Disputing this is like putting up a fight with the One who has called and anointed them.

If a prophet falls, please pray for him. If a prophet sins against you, please do not take the law into your own hands, but rather see him to resolve the matter; if he does not listen to you, bring in someone to whom he is likely to listen and speak to him; if he still does not listen, take the matter to the church and, if he does not listen to the church, let the church declare him an infidel. Then, you may deal with him as you may do with any simple person out there.

GEN 20:1-7

And Abraham journeyed from there to the South, and dwelt between Kadesh and Shur, and stayed in Gerar. Now Abraham said of Sarah his wife, "She is my sister". And Abimelech king of Gerar sent and took Sarah. But God came to Abimelech in a dream by night, and said to him, "Indeed you are a dead man because of the woman whom you have taken, for she is a man's wife". But Abimelech had not come near her; and he said, "Lord, will You slay a righteous nation also? Did he not say to me, 'She is my sister'? And she, even she herself said, 'He is my brother'. In the integrity of my heart and innocence of my hands I have done this." And God said to him in a dream, "Yes, I know that you did this in the integrity of your heart. For I also withheld you from sinning against Me; therefore I did not let you touch her. Now therefore, restore the man's wife; for he is a prophet, and he will pray for you and you shall live. But if you do not restore her, know that you shall surely die, you and all who are yours."

The above scripture speaks of the story of Abraham and Abimelech, the King of Gerar, regarding Sarah, Abraham's wife. The Bible says that Abraham lied to the king that his wife was merely his sister. The king then took her as one of his wives, and gave Abraham, the supposed brother, a lot of wealth and possessions. But the night that the king wanted to be intimate with her, God spoke to him, that he dare not touch her because she was a married woman. The king told God that he was not aware that she was a married woman, for Abraham had told him that she was his sister. God replied that He knew, which is why He had not yet struck him.

Then, God asked him to go to Abraham for prayer that He might not kill him (v.7): *"Now therefore, restore the man's wife; for he is a prophet, and he will pray for you and you shall live. But if you do not restore her, know that you shall surely die, you and all who are yours."*

I always wonder why God sent this poor king to Abraham to be prayed for, knowing that Abraham was in the wrong and had lied to him. This may not sit well for those who are reading this story; it seems like God Himself was Abraham's accomplice to rob this king, but it was not so. God has His own way of handling things when it comes to His servants, the prophets. To implicate yourself in the business of prophets is to interfere with God's way of doing things, and that will definitely lead to great trouble. Do not harm prophets of the Lord, no matter what.

Never Judge Your Prophet – Seek the Lord Concerning Him

As it is easy to judge things that you do not understand, things that you cannot rationally master, so it is easy to judge prophets, because it is almost impossible to keep up with them. Prophets do not operate on the level of sense but rather on the level of the Spirit. The realm of

Spirit and spiritual things does not always make sense to the natural mind. Thus, it is easy to find yourself judging the prophet on what he might have said, might have done, and where he might have gone. So you should beware.

When someone does not know anything about you, they easily make speculations. Many speculate about prophets and build opinions about them that are simply unfounded. Elijah asked the widow of Zarephath to bring him water and to make him a cake in a time of drought, which may have come across as insensitive and manipulative. Especially as she told him that her supplies were limited, and she needed to make a cake so that she and her son might eat a last meal before dying, it might seem that Elijah deserves rebuke: "Stop taking advantage of this poor dying widow. You are a man; go out there and fend for yourself." Or another critic may have said, "Prophets of nowadays are simple crooks and thieves who feed off the poor and the weak. Look at this so-called Elijah, how he is trying to survive this drought by taking from this poor widow and her son!"

Many people might have judged Elijah because of the ways that God expresses Himself through His servants, the prophets. These ways are indeed not our ways and we will never be able to comprehend them fully. Prophets may sometimes do things that might be shocking, things that your reasoning mind may disapprove of or immediately reject, but I plead with you to pull yourself together and never to judge the prophet. Just seek the Lord concerning them.

Isa 20:2-4

At the same time the LORD spoke by Isaiah the son of Amoz, saying, "Go, and remove the sackcloth from your body, and take your sandals off your feet". And he did so, walking naked and barefoot. Then the LORD said, "Just as My servant Isaiah has walked naked

> and barefoot three years *for* a sign and a wonder against Egypt and Ethiopia, so shall the king of Assyria lead away the Egyptians as prisoners and the Ethiopians as captives, young and old, naked and barefoot, with their buttocks uncovered, to the shame of Egypt".

This interesting scripture seems to be in total contradiction to the laws of Moses. The law considered nakedness to be sacred and one ought not to be exposed. In the above text, God is asking His servant to do something that was clearly outside the norms of culture and against the law. God asked Isaiah to minister the Word of God while being naked for three good years. Can you imagine your pastor walking into church topless and barefoot on a Sunday morning? There probably wouldn't be a church service that day as everyone would be preoccupied with how to help the pastor, who had gone mad and was prancing around, undressed. I bet that pastor would end up in a mental institution. And if such general reactions might occur were people to see their pastor topless in the church, how shocking would it be for the people around Isaiah to observe him preaching the Word of God, while completely naked and barefoot! Havoc must have occurred in the community, city, and the nation of Israel at large.

It is difficult to understand prophets and their ministries, but understanding them is not a prerequisite for accepting and standing with them. Our attitude when we are troubled by the ministerial actions of the prophet should be to seek God concerning them. If they are operating in the flesh and not in the Spirit, the Lord will caution you and will redress them.

Support Your Prophet

There are two key areas of your support that are indispensable: to *provide for him* and to *protect and defend him*.

Provide for him

It is heaven's expectation that you feed your own prophet; by doing so you attract great blessings into your own life. You can only make demands on the anointing that you support and only the anointing that you support can sustain you. To support your prophet is a secret for invoking the blessings of God into your life, but it is also a noble assignment. You function as an extended hand from the Lord Himself, which supports His servant.

> ### 2 Kgs 4:8-10
>
> Now it happened one day that Elisha went to Shunem, where there was a notable woman, and she persuaded him to eat some food. So it was, as often as he passed by, he would turn in there to eat some food. And she said to her husband, "Look now, I know that this *is* a holy man of God, who passes by us regularly. Please, let us make a small upper room on the wall; and let us put a bed for him there, and a table and a chair and a lampstand; so it will be, whenever he comes to us, he can turn there."

In this passage from the Bible, a woman from Shunem saw Elisha with his servant, passing near them often. She persuaded him to stop by her house to have something to eat. This turned into a habit for Elisha and his servant. Whenever they passed through her town, they would stop by her house for something to eat. It did not stop at that. After some time, she asked her husband's permission to build and furnish an upper room for Elisha so that whenever he came to eat, he might also have a place to rest and relax.

The actions of this woman are what we should replicate today in taking care of our prophets. A well-cared-for prophet will surely be a blessing to you, but a neglected prophet, one left to himself, may not be a great source of blessings – not because he is unable to bless you

The Rise of the Prophetic Voice

but because your lack of support for him will be a barrier. Because the woman of Shunem supported Elisha, the prophet, he asked what could be done for her, what her need was, that God might meet it right there, because of her kind heart towards the prophet. Elisha gave her a blank cheque so that she could state her request. Although she refused to give a personal request, Elisha learned from his servant that she did not have any children. So he prophesied that she would become a mother, the following year at around the same time.

Her blessings did not come merely because of need. I believe that there were many women in the same city who had no children. They did not receive the same miracle and blessing. Her miracle came specifically because of her kind heart towards a *man of God*. Her deed made way for her miracle.

Protect and defend

Prophets are the targets of many forces out there; it is imperative that you understand your role in protecting and defending your prophet. Most believers leave this role to God and His angels: they fold their hands when their prophet is falsely accused, dragged in the mud, abused, ill-treated or stoned, hoping that by some mysterious happenings, God will intervene. They completely forget that God intervenes through them, and if they fold their hands and do not stand with the prophet, their man of God, the enemy will cause him great pain.

A man of God turned bitter toward his congregation after he had been through great pain and attacks of all sorts on social media, radio and TV; people got physical with him while the people in his church were quiet. They watched him go through his ordeal alone. His bitterness was due to his disappointment in being left alone in his terrible moment of pain. Please be reminded that your man of God is still a man and, though he is representing God and working for him, he still feels pain and disappointment. You need to stand with him and be a point of courage for him in difficult days, which are many for prophets.

The time will come when we will not remember the insults of our enemies but the silence of our friends.

Pray for your prophet

We often feel that our prophets do not need our prayers; they are too spiritual and close to God to be in need of our prayers. This is a dangerous and unbiblical way of thinking. No matter how spiritual your prophet may be, please remember that he is not God and still needs your prayers.

In Acts 12:5-17, the Bible tells us the story of Peter while in prison; because Christ and the church were praying for his well-being, God heard and sent an angel at night to set him free. Peter was considered the first apostle in the New Testament, and not just because he was the oldest of the twelve who accompanied Jesus Christ during his ministry on earth. Rather, Christ had given the keys of the kingdom of God to Peter; it is he who preached the first sermon after the outpouring of the Holy Spirit that saw three thousand new converts in the Body of Christ.

Though Peter was the first apostle of the first church, when he was under attack and persecution the church prayed for him. They did not say, "Who are we to pray for such a great man?" or, "He is already too big in the Lord and close to God to require our prayers. God Himself will intervene for him without our prayers." Just as the church prayed for Peter, it is important that you pray for your prophet.

---

1 Cor 16:9

For a great and effective door has opened to me, and *there are* many adversaries.

The Rise of the Prophetic Voice

Here, Paul is requesting that the church pray for him in view of the ministerial opportunities that are in front of him. This should tell you that praying for your man of God is important; I encourage you to do so. Pray for your prophet not to fall into temptation; pray for him to remain faithful to God, pray for him to keep on growing in God more and more; pray for his family, for his health, for his protection; pray that he may remain really connected to God.

CHAPTER TEN

RIGHT ATTITUDE TOWARDS PROPHECY

Do Not Despise It

The prophetic is a ministry that is purely based on the supernatural ability that God gives His servant, and this ministry is not in any way whatsoever based on talents, skills or man's mere efforts. Since it is a ministry based purely on supernatural ability, the prophetic is impossible to understand with a carnal mind. As a result, many are sceptical and sometimes resentful towards the supernatural gift of prophecy.

There are many sentimentsin the world regarding the prophetic, and most of those sentiments are simply based on the fact of our limited minds. Many try to understand the operation of the prophetic with their minds and, as they quickly discover, the prophetic does not make sense to their minds. So, they turn against it.

I have seen and heard of ministers of the gospel who preach in their sermons to stay away from the prophetic; they go out of their way to undermine and denigrate the prophetic. Along with them, many in the Body of Christ and in the world today feel that to stay away from the prophetic is to tread wisely, because to them the prophetic is controversial. They see no logic in it, and some bluntly call it trickery, staged, and fake. They believe that the prophetic, and other supernatural gifts, operates by magic and diabolical powers. So, they despise and spurn it.

> **1 THESS 5:20**
>
> Do not despise prophecies.

The Bible irrevocably instructs us not to despise prophecies. Irrespective of your personal sentiments towards the prophetic, or any bad experience you may have had in the past with false prophecies, if you want to be a child God who is in right standing with the Lord, you should not despise prophecies.

Examine It

> **1 THESS 5:21-22**
>
> Test all things; hold fast what is good. Abstain from every form of evil.

Though we are to *examine prophecy*, we are not to examine the Word that comes from God Himself. God's Word is perfect. We are not wise enough to correct Him. We are instructed to *examine prophecy*, not to correct what God is saying to us, but rather to test if it is really the Word of God. When we are convinced that the word of prophecy is not a made-up word, invented or imagined by a mere man, we will still need to scrutinise the prophecy to ensure that the true Word of the Lord is not mixed up with the added input of the prophet, through whom that Word is given.

Our attitude while examining a prophetic word should not be scepticism, for that will translate into being spiteful towards prophecy. Our attitude should be one of openness to the Holy Spirit

The Rise of the Prophetic Voice

of God so that the Spirit may guide us. But how should we examine prophecy? We are to examine prophecies through the written Word of God and through the Holy Spirit. It is true that not everything, about which God speaks to us will be found in the Bible, chapter and verse. Yet, we will know that the prophecy is not in contradiction with the Word of God and, though the biblical confirmation may not necessarily be written, the confirmation will be evident by the *spirit of the Scriptures.*

MARK 9:40

For he who is not against us is on our side.

Beside the written Word, we all examine prophecies by the Holy Spirit, and prayer comes in very handy here. The Bible says that the Holy Spirit will guide us in all truth (John 16:13).

Often, you will receive an immediate witness in your spirit that a prophecy given to you is from God; the Holy Spirit will make sure that He confirms to your spirit that it is from Him, and in those cases you do not need to ask Him again about it.

JOHN 10:27

My sheep hear My voice, and I know them, and they follow Me.

You will recognise the voice of the Lord, your God, through the prophecy. When you are not sure about the prophet prophesying, or the prophecy itself does not completely flow well with you, you should not despise that prophecy. Instead, examine whether it is from God or whether the genuine Word of God may be mixed with the unnecessary input of the prophet, whose input comes from the flesh rather than the Spirit. Please note that I have specified the *flesh of the prophet*, because the input of the prophet is not bad in itself, as long as the Holy Spirit inspires it. The problem arises when the prophet's unwarranted emotions, views, and conclusions come to play a role in the prophecy, thus creating biases and distorting the Word given to him from God.

Believe It

> ### ROM 4:18
>
> [Abraham] who, contrary to hope, in hope believed, so that he became the father of many nations, according to what was spoken, "So shall your descendants be".

> ### 2 KGS 7:1-2
>
> Then Elisha said, "Hear the word of the Lord. Thus says the Lord: 'Tomorrow about this time a seah of fine flour shall be sold for a shekel, and two seahs of barley for a shekel, at the gate of Samaria'." So an officer on whose hand the king leaned answered the man of God and said, "Look, if the Lord would make windows in heaven, could this thing be?"
> And he said, "In fact, you shall see it with your eyes, but you shall not eat of it."

You will not see the manifestation of a prophetic word that you have not believed, unless it falls into the category of the prophecies that require no man's input, such as the prophecy about the Second Coming of Christ; whether you believe it or not, the Second Coming will still come to pass. But, for most of your direct prophecies, they will be activated through your faith.

The patriarch Abraham had to believe God that His Word in his life would come to pass, though naturally the prophesied event was impossible. He was old and his wife Sarah had passed her childbearing time; she was already in menopause. Still, Abraham did not stop believing that God's Word would to come to pass. So, God turned Sarah's menopause to a *meno-play*; she conceived and gave birth to Isaac, the promised son.

In 2 Kgs 7:1-2, the officer on whose arm the king leaned did not believe the prophetic word from Elisha, the prophet. The man of God told him that he would see that prophecy fulfilled for others but he would not benefit from it because he did not himself believe it. He died as the prophecy was fulfilled. When you receive a prophetic word, it is important that you believe it and wait for its manifestation in complete faith.

Doubting a prophetic word given to you is never a way to activate its manifestation in your life. I have heard people to whom God had given a prophetic word say, "I will wait and see if this will really come to pass". They say this as a way for them to dare God to prove them wrong and to fulfil the prophecy He gave to them; unfortunately, time and time again, we see that daring God in this way does not work.

HAB 2:3

For the vision is yet for an appointed time; but at the end it will speak, and it will not lie. Though it tarries, wait for it; because it will surely come, it will not tarry.

The vision referred to above by Habakkuk is a prophetic message that came through an open vision. He is exhorting people to believe, that the thing envisioned will surely come to pass. Though it may tarry, the vision will still come to pass. The prophet models the attitude of faith that we should adopt towards the prophetic word, which we receive from the Lord.

Obey and Apply It

> ### 2 Kgs 5:10-14
>
> And Elisha sent a messenger to him, saying, "Go and wash in the Jordan seven times, and your flesh shall be restored to you, and you shall be clean". But Naaman became furious, and went away and said, "Indeed, I said to myself, 'He will surely come out to me, and stand and call on the name of the Lord his God, and wave his hand over the place, and heal the leprosy'. Are not the Abanah and the Pharpar, the rivers of Damascus, better than all the waters of Israel? Could I not wash in them and be clean?" So he turned and went away in a rage. And his servant came near and spoke to him, and said, "My father, if the prophet had told you to do something great, would you not have done it? How much more then, when he says to you, 'Wash, and be clean'?" So he went down and dipped seven times in the Jordan, according to the saying of the man of God; and his flesh was restored like the flesh of a little child, and he was clean.

Should the prophetic word given to you come with an instruction for you to obey, you should quickly obey it or forget the manifestation of that prophecy in your life. I encourage you, whenever you receive a prophetic word, to always ask yourself if there is in it an instruction to obey or something to immediately apply in your life. Pray that the Lord may enlighten you about any instruction in the prophetic word.

In the above scripture, Elisha gave Naaman, the Syrian, an instruction to dip himself seven times in the River Jordan and he would be healed of leprosy. He was reluctant at first to obey this word, but after his servant spoke to him he obeyed the prophetic instruction and received his miracle. Can you imagine if he had not obeyed the prophetic instruction given to him? He would have surely missed his miracle.

Every prophetic instruction obeyed paves a way to a new dimension. As you obey the prophetic instruction given to you, God will fulfil His part of the bargain. So do not tarry. Obey what is instructed to you by God in the prophetic.

Pray for His Fulfilment

> ### DAN 9:1-2
>
> In the first year of Darius the son of Ahasuerus, of the lineage of the Medes, who was made king over the realm of the Chaldeans. In the first year of his reign I, Daniel, understood by the books the number of the years *specified* by the word of the LORD through Jeremiah the prophet, that he would accomplish seventy years in the desolations of Jerusalem.

> ### DAN 10:12-14
>
> Then he said to me, "Do not fear, Daniel, for from the first day that you set your heart to understand, and to humble yourself before your God, your words were heard; and I have come because of your words. But the prince of the kingdom of Persia withstood me twenty-one days; and behold, Michael, one of the chief princes, came to help me, for I had been left alone there with the kings of Persia. Now I have come to make you understand what will happen to your people in the latter days, for the vision *refers* to many days yet to come."

It is very important, in the manifestation of your prophetic word, that you remain in prayer for it. Daniel prayed earnestly to God for the fulfilment of a long-awaited manifestation of the prophetic. For twenty-one days he fasted and prayed that the prophetic word in his life might come to pass. Jesus Christ Himself instructed His disciples to remain in Jerusalem in prayer until the prophecy of the outpouring of the Holy Spirit was fulfilled in their lives. So, the disciples waited in prayer for the manifestation of the promise (Acts 1:8).

Praying for the manifestation of your prophetic word is critical for two essential reasons. First, by praying for your prophetic word, you remain in the presence of God and keep your spirit aligned with Him. This will facilitate your receiving the manifestation of your prophetic word. Secondly, by praying for your prophetic word, you will deal with every contrary spirit and evil force that may work against its fulfilment.

Seal it in your life continuously with your praise, your confession, and your seed offering. This is what I personally do without fail: I seal the prophetic word that I receive in my life with my praise, confession of faith, and my seed offering. Once I receive a prophetic word, I begin to praise God continually for it to manifest soon. I praise Him for giving me the word but I praise also in anticipation of its manifestation.

> O Lord, I thank You for this prophetic word. Thank You for telling me that I shall receive ... this or that... I shall become ...this or that... I shall see ... this or that... I know You could have given this word to anyone out there but You chose me and for this I praise your Holy Name. And Lord I also praise You because in Your faithfulness, You will surely fulfil that which Your mouth has declared.

I praise Him continually, until the manifestation of the prophecy. I strongly advise that you write down the prophecies you receive so that you may systematically learn to praise God for each one of them. Not only should you keep praising God for your prophetic word, but you should also learn to confess the manifestation of your prophecy in your life and to align your spirit to receive it.

> ### HEB 10:23
>
> Let us hold fast the confession of *our* hope without wavering, for He who promised *is* faithful.

You must keep confessing that your prophecy will come to pass. Keep speaking it into manifestation and you shall see it come to pass. Lastly, I make sure that I seal every prophetic word I receive with a prophetic seed offering, not only when I receive that prophetic word but even thereafter. I keep sowing seed offerings towards the prophetic word. This offering will help us to quickly see the manifestation of the prophetic word.

Conclusion

We are in an era where God is restoring His prophetic voice in the church and in the world at large. Men and women from all walks of life are being used in the prophetic to bring about the light and power of God in these end times. There is an indisputable rising of the prophetic voice in our times, today, which is happening in alignment with prophecy of old, the prophecy of Joel.

> ### JOEL 2:28
>
> And it shall come to pass afterward that I will pour out My Spirit on all flesh; your sons and your daughters shall prophesy, your old men shall dream dreams, your young men shall see visions.

The arising of the prophetic voice betokens the prophetic movement occurring in the church and in the world today. Unfortunately, the Body of Christ is no longer as knowledgeable about the prophetic as it was in the olden days. Therefore, people are largely still sceptical towards the prophetic. The prophetic, which we see today around the world, is certainly the working of the Holy Spirit, which cannot be stopped, no matter what. The prophetic ministry is the end-time ministry and indispensable to the agenda of God for the world now. I sincerely believe that the prophetic is the main weapon in the Lord's hand for the last harvest of souls.

Though not everyone is called to become a prophet of the Lord, everyoneiscalled at least to participate in the prophetic, irrespective of their calling and assignment. Embrace the prophetic and do not fight it, for you will cause yourself harm and be on the wrong side of history. The arising of the prophetic should include you and not render you irrelevant in such times as our own.

As one of the pioneers of the prophetic movement in my own times, the Holy Spirit has vividly given me an assignment, to pray and to impart the prophetic grace provided to me, so that it may be distributed to as many as He will send to me. As you read this book, I pray:

I pray that the prophetic anointing of God may begin to work in you in the name of Jesus. I pray that your spiritual eyes may open to see the visions of the Lord, and that your spiritual ears may open to hear the voice of God, accurately for your life and for the benefit of others. I pray that from this day forth you may begin to flow accurately in the prophetic in the name of Jesus Christ, our Lord and Saviour. Amen.

Shalom

NOTES

NOTES

_____

_____

_____

_____

_____

_____

_____

_____

_____

_____

_____

_____

_____

NOTES

_____

_____

_____

_____

_____

_____

_____

_____

_____

_____

_____

_____

Alph Lukau

NOTES

The Rise of the Prophetic Voice

BOOKS BY ALPH LUKAU

Overcoming the Devourer

The Lord directed me to write the truth about the *devourer* so that His people may be completely released from the traps of this monster. God's people are dying not because of lack of power or anointing, nor lack of motivation or life resolutions, but simply because of lack of knowledge.

Knowledge is a tool that not only determines life or death, but also how far one goes in life. As children of the Most High God, we should be the most vigilant people in constantly seeking knowledge that contributes to our well being in Christ.

This book will open your eyes to the truth regarding the *devourer* who has been destroying your God-given crops and the joy of the Lord in your life. This truth shall set your life free. You will recover all that has been stolen from you so that you may begin to see the fulfilment of the promises of God in your life.

****

The Cure

I have received from the Lord a special revelation and grace that I would like to share with you in this book. This book will lead you to discover that God has been trying to heal you all this while. He cares enough for you. His joy is to see you again in good health and prosperous.

When we speak of a cure, we are referring to a remedy or an antidote that will eradicate, eliminate, destroy and remove every sickness and disease from your body.

In this book, "the cure" refers to the healing power of the Holy Ghost in a dimension that many have not yet experienced, whether or not we belong to the Body of Christ.

****

OFFICIAL PAGES

Facebook AlphLuaku01

Instagram

Alph Lukau

Twitter @Alph Lukau

YouTube Pastor Alph Lukau

Website www.alphlukau.com

Printed in the United States
By Bookmasters